Old Fashioned Children's Games

Old Fashioned Children's Games

Over 200 Outdoor, Car Trip, Song, Card and Party Activities

by
SHARON O'BRYAN

Drawings by Mary Anne Fitzgerald

McFarland & Company, Inc., Publishers
Jefferson, North Carolina, and London

Front cover: Artwork by Mary Anne Fitzgerald.

6 05 9804

British Library Cataloguing-in-Publication data are available

Library of Congress Cataloguing-in-Publication Data

O'Bryan, Sharon (Sharon Elizabeth)
    Old fashioned children's games : over 200 outdoor, car trip, song,
card and party activities / by Sharon O'Bryan ; drawings by Mary
Anne Fitzgerald.
        p.   cm.
    Includes index.
    ISBN 0-7864-0558-9 (sewn softcover : 55# alkaline paper) ∞
    1. Games.   2. Outdoor games.   3. Singing games.   I. Title.
GV1203.03   1999
790.1— dc21   98-37436
                                                           CIP

Manufactured in the United States of America

*McFarland & Company, Inc., Publishers
    Box 611, Jefferson, North Carolina 28640*

I dedicate this book
to the beautiful memory of our 21-year-old son,
John Thomas O'Bryan.

A senior at Rose Hulman University in Indiana, John was on his way to tutor students the morning he was killed in a car and train accident at an unguarded crossing with malfunctioning crossing lights. It was the day before he was to come home for Christmas break. Five months later, we accepted his two summa cum laude degrees, one in mathematics and the other in physics, both awarded to him posthumously.

John carried a 4.0 grade point average each year he attended Rose Hulman, was the top-ranked student all four years and won numerous awards, plaques and trophies for outstanding achievements of merit. John presented five different papers at six mathematical conferences held at various universities throughout the United States during his college career. His most outstanding work was featured at a special session of the MAA held in San Francisco the fall before his death.

Although John possessed amazing brilliance, his intelligence wasn't his greatest characteristic. His humor, goodness and constant willingness to help others are what people who knew John remember most about him.

John's indomitable spirit urged me on and wouldn't let me rest until I had this book published. His enthusiasm, love of life and consistent example of completing every task he ever attempted were the forces that drove me after his death.

This book is a tribute to his happiness, his zest for living and the enjoyment he experienced in everything he did, including playing old-fashioned children's games when he was a child. I hope these games will bring smiles to kids' faces — like his unforgettable smile, etched in my heart forever.

Acknowledgments

Special thanks to:

• Steve, our outstanding son, who consistently provided crucial help setting up my computer, listened to my pathetic wails on the phone when I thought my files had gotten wiped out and always created miracles regaining files I thought I'd lost.

• Carol Decker, my sister, who worked tirelessly hand-scoring the music, asking nothing in return.

• Scott Weinhold, who edited, formatted and transcribed the musical scores, providing the all-important professional-looking musical accompaniments.

• Mary Anne Fitzgerald, the illustrator, who did a fantastic job on the artwork, refusing payment for the many hours she spent perfecting it.

• Mom, who continuously sympathized and who encouraged me not to give up.

• Tom, my husband, who gave me the all-important financial freedom and security necessary to proceed with this book. Using patience and humor, he read game after game and acted as consultant.

Table of Contents

Car Games

Card Games

Singing Games and Campfire Songs

Party Games

Introductory Note

What's happened to old-fashioned children's games? For centuries kids delighted in games of all sorts — running and jumping games, guessing games, singing games. These games were an integral part of their physical and psychological development.

Over the past few decades, electronic and computer games have all but taken over. Now, old-fashioned games are in danger of becoming a thing of the past. Although modern computer and electronic games provide some mental stimulation, they don't encourage camaraderie, physical activity, coordination and social interaction as old-fashioned games do. If the games of earlier years are not taught to kids of this generation, a loved and cherished tradition will vanish from the American scene.

This book contains a collection of old-fashioned games for children from two to twelve years old. This collection includes five categories: Outside Games, Car Games, Card Games, Singing Games and Campfire Songs, and Party Games. Many of these games stimulate imagination, increase self-confidence, and develop memory skills. However, the main object of this book is to generate good old-fashioned fun for kids.

While compiling this book, I experienced tinges of nostalgia for my childhood years in a small town in Indiana. I still remember the giddy thrill of playing Kick the Can or Hide and Seek on steamy summer nights. I'll never forget the rush of excitement I felt lying on a bed of freshly fallen snow, creating snow angels. As you use this book playing with kids, I hope it will rekindle a few fond memories of your childhood. Have fun!

Outside
Games

Angels in the Snow

Over the years, children have delighted in this wintertime pastime. There is no winner or loser. Children lie down with their backs against the untrodden snow and spread out their arms and legs as far as possible, pushing away the snow beneath them. The resulting impressions look like angels lying in the snow.

Boys and girls may decorate the "angels," using their imagination to create a face. Unshelled walnuts, marbles or charcoal are good for eyes; a small plum or piece of carrot can be a nose and a sliced cherry or strawberry makes a mouth. Kids can add sparkling garlands to the angel wings.

Balloon Toss

Everyone has a wild and wet time playing this old favorite, which involves lots of giggling and screaming. Two groups line up standing about five feet apart, facing each other. Players standing directly across from each other are a pair. Each pair is given a balloon filled with water. On the signal "One, two, three, throw!" the player holding the water balloon must toss it to the partner.

If the balloon falls to the ground but doesn't burst, the partner may pick it up and wait for the next throw. After each throw, players must take two steps backward. If a pair's balloon bursts, one of them gets soaked, and that pair is out. Play continues until only one pair is left — the winners.

Bear and Beasts

This exciting chase game is great for a large number of boys and girls. One player, who is *bear,* stands in the middle of a wide circle of players. *Bear* points to each player as quickly as possible, assigning every one an animal name, for example, lion, giraffe, gorilla, monkey, elephant, zebra, etc. Then *bear* calls out the names of two, saying, "Monkey, chase giraffe." The player who is monkey must run around the circle chasing the giraffe. *Bear* steps into the monkey's place in the circle. (In this example, the monkey is the chaser and the giraffe is the runner.)

If the chaser tags the runner before he or she has run around the circle and back to his or her own place, the chaser takes the runner's place in the circle and the runner is then *bear* in the next round. If the runner gets back safely to his or her spot in the circle, the chaser is the next *bear.* Then the new *bear* bestows different animal names to all the children and they must remember them in the next round.

As the game continues, there is a lot of laughter because players become confused after being given so many different animal names that they may forget their name in a round and get a late start or run at the wrong time. This game keeps kids entertained for hours.

Bird, Beast or Fish

This enchanting game is a winner with older children. Players sit in a circle, and one player sits in the center holding a rubber ball. Before the ball is thrown, this player says, "Bird, beast or fish," and quickly throws the ball at one of the other players. As the ball is being thrown, the center player also calls out one of these words and counts to 10. For example, center player cries, "Bird, beast or fish," and then states "Beast" (or either of the other choices) and counts to 10. The player catching the ball must quickly name a beast, such as "lion."

The same "bird, beast or fish" can be named only once, which makes the game harder as it continues. Any player who can't name what was requested before the count of 10 has a point counted against him or her. At the end of approximately 20 minutes, the player with the least amount of counts against him or her wins.

Birds

A modern-day version of a centuries-old game, this is a fun tag game in which kids act as *birds*. Players stand in a circle, with one player designated as the *seller* in the middle. Another player, the *buyer*, stands outside the circle, outside of hearing distance. *Seller* stands in front of the birds, asking what bird they wish to be. Each player picks a different bird they wish to be: starling, cardinal, robin, turtle dove, woodpecker, etc. *Buyer* returns and asks, "Have you any birds for sale?" *Seller* responds, "Yes." *Buyer* asks, "Blue jays?" *Seller* responds, "No!"

This questioning continues until *buyer* correctly guesses a *bird* named among the players. Then all players cry "Yes!" and the *bird* named darts off around the circle as fast as a fleeting rabbit, trying either to get back to his or her place before being tagged by *buyer* or before *buyer* assumes the player's place in the circle.

If the *buyer* beats the "named bird" back to his or her place in the circle, the "named bird" becomes the new *buyer*, and the game starts all over as in the beginning. If the "named bird" returns to his or her spot in the circle before being tagged by the *buyer*, he or she is safe; the *buyer* makes another guess as to what birds are for sale, etc. Player may take turns acting as the *seller*. This game increases children's awareness of birds and provides an exciting tag game.

Chain

Many years ago, this thrilling tag game was particularly adored by children six years of age and up. A large number of kids is needed for this invigorating pastime — a greater number of players definitely adds increased delight. The game is a terrific choice for company picnics or on the school playground where kids are eager for a good time. It's different because when the player who is *it* tags another player, that child has to join hands with *it* and from then on they run together.

Every boy or girl tagged joins the chasers, taking the hand of the player who touched him or her, thereby creating an ever-lengthening chain of chasers. Players can be tagged only by a chaser's disengaged hand (i.e., the outside hand of a child at one or the other end of the chain). When ten or more players are linked together, they make a frightful-looking predator. Fortunately for those who are still untagged, the longer the chain grows, the clumsier and slower it moves, making it more prone to breaking as the two ends try to tag different players.

If the chain is broken, a child can't be caught and chasers must first join hands again. Free players may charge the chain, aiming at the weakest link, attempting to break through before a player on either end of the chain tags them. The last player caught always feels elated and proud at having evaded the chain the longest and gets to be *it* in the next game, forming a new chain as chasing starts once again.

Chinese Ball

This game is lots of fun when the ball is passed as quickly as possible. At least ten players are needed. All the players stand in a circle except one, who stands in the center with a ball and tosses it to any player who tries to catch it. Players on the catcher's right side and left side must both raise their left arms.

When a player raises the wrong arm or raises his or her arm when the ball is not caught by someone next to him or her, that player must leave the circle. If a player fails to catch a ball thrown at him or her, that player must also leave the circle. The game goes on until there are only three players left. They win the game.

Circle Relay

Boys and girls love this relay game. At least ten players are needed. Children divide into equal teams and stand five feet behind each other in even rows. On the signal "Go," the first one in line on each team races to the right side of his or her team, comes bake up the left side and runs up and tags the second one in that line. Immediately, that player runs to the end of the line in the same way and tags the third child in line, and the game continues.

Players who have taken a turn wait while other players continue to play. The first team that completes the task of having each member of the team tagged following the above rules wins the game.

Circle Tag

This exciting tag game is a winner with youngsters. Players form a circle, standing about five feet from the player on either side. The *leader* stands outside the circle; on his or her signal "Go," all the children run, trying to pass the player on the right. Runners must run in the pattern of the circle. When a player catches up with the one in front of him or her and tags that player, that player is out. The *leader* may call, "Reverse." Then players have to quickly turn around and run the other way. The last player left in the circle wins.

Come and Get It

An adult normally hides the "loot" outside — behind bushes or trees, under the deck and on the porch. The items hidden could be marbles, rocks painted a certain color, pennies or any number of items of your choice. The better the hiding places, the more exciting the game is. The children hide their eyes as the objects are being hidden.

After all the loot is hidden, the hider shouts, "Come and get it!" Then all the kids attempt to find as many of the items as possible. The one who finds the most at the end of approximately ten minutes wins. That child may be awarded a small prize.

Cross Tag

This exciting game of tag adds a different slant to the game. The player chosen *it* starts running after another player. A third player in the game may rush across *its* path; at that point *it* is obliged to chase the interrupting player. This continues until *it* tags someone. It's much more exciting when players try to slow *it* down by silly horseplay. They don't necessarily have to cross between *it* and the player he or she is chasing. This all adds to the confusion of this fun chase game.

Do This, Do That

Kids love this game, which is similar to Follow the Leader. The *leader* says, "Do this," and all the other players must follow the *leader's* actions. Whenever the *leader* says, "*Do that,*" and performs a feat, players should not do as the *leader*. Players who follow the *leader's* action at that time are out. It's a lively game, especially if the *leader* is fast-acting.

Dodge Ball

This active outdoor game is lots of fun when played with a large number of kids (ten or more). There are several ways to play. In this variation, children form into two groups. One group forms a large circle — the larger the circle, the better. The other group stands within the circle, in no particular formation.

The circle players try to hit the center players with a rubber playground ball, volley ball or beach ball. Those throwing the ball should aim low to prevent others from getting hurt. The center players dodge to avoid being hit. They may dodge, stoop, jump or run to escape the ball, but they may not leave the ring.

Players hit on any part of the body at once join the circle players. If two center players are hit by one throw of the ball, only the first one joins the circle players. Circle players regain the ball either by a toss from a center player or by a circle player stepping in for the ball if it is not within reach. The last player in the center is the winner. Then the circle players become the center players and vice versa.

Dress Up

This too is an activity that kids have relished for hundreds of years. Small girls and boys particularly like to while away the time playing this. A box filled with old clothes, shoes, hats and jewelry is needed. Kids love to play Dress Up because it gives them a chance to pretend to be someone else and also to act out different roles in society. They may choose to be a teacher, parent, doctor, minister, lawyer, nurse, pilot, etc. Children rarely get bored with this one.

Fast Act

Boys and girls love this game. The player who is *it* stands in the center of a circle formed by the others seated on the ground. While constantly making gestures and moves, the seated players toss a scarf, handkerchief or ball from one player to another. *It* tries to touch the object thrown while the object is in midair. If *it* succeeds, the last player to throw becomes the new *it*.

Flower Jewelry

It's not certain how many hundreds of years kids have had a ball with this creative pastime. All that is needed is a field of flowering clovers, wildflowers or dandelions. After children have learned how to tie a knot, they enjoy this amusement. Normally, girls like to play it up to an older age than boys. Children pick the flowers. Then they sit on the ground and tie the flowers together, making flower bracelets, necklaces, rings or head wreaths.

Kids not only adorn themselves with the flower jewelry but also make enough to take home for other members of their family. If an adult leads this expedition to the field, it's a great opportunity for kids to learn the names of wildflowers.

Follow the Leader

For many years, children have had a fun time playing this simple game. Players line up in a row behind the player acting as the *leader* and follow whatever actions the *leader* performs — skipping, jumping, singing, dancing, turning somersaults or cartwheels, hopping on one foot, etc. Whenever players don't follow the *leader's* actions, they go to the back of the line. After a certain amount of time, the second child in line becomes the new *leader*, until each player has taken a turn as the *leader*. Children have lots of fun when this game is played on a playground that has swings, slides, teeter-totters and monkey bars.

Fox and Geese

This fantastic, old-fashioned variation of tag, which requires four or more players, can be played on the pavement or in a field of snow. If playing in the snow, one player trudges through untrodden snow, carefully drawing the playing area. When playing on pavement, the players start by drawing a chalk circle approximately 20 to 50 feet around. Draw another, small circle in the center. This is the *fox's* den and should be large enough to hold all the players.

Eight even pie-shaped sections are drawn from the middle circle to the outer circle. One player is chosen as *fox*. The other players are *geese*. As the game begins, *fox* stands in the den while all the *geese* stand on the outside line of the circle. After a signal is sounded to start, *fox* races from the den down one of the lines toward the outer circle, trying to catch the *geese*. All players, including *fox*, must stay on the lines. If *fox* steps off a line when he or she tags one of the *geese*, it doesn't count. Whenever *fox* tags a player or a player steps off any of the lines, that player must go to the *fox's* den.

To make the game more exciting, you can make a rule that any captured goose can be released from the den by being tagged by an uncaptured *goose*. The last *goose* to be captured is the next *fox*.

Gypsy

Little girls squeal with glee playing this combination hide-and-seek/tag game. One girl is *mother*, one is *gypsy* and the rest of the players are the *children*. *Mother* turns around and covers her eyes while *gypsy* hides each of the *children*, one by one, in different places. After the last one is hidden, *mother* searches to find them as *gypsy* stays and waits for all of the *children* to be found. Then *mother* and *children* chase the *gypsy*. The first one to tag the *gypsy* is *gypsy* in the next game. Players can take turns acting as *mother*.

Hang Tag

In this variation of tag, players cannot be tagged when they have their feet off the ground. *It* chases players, who try to avoid being tagged by jumping up to hang on a tree branch or by climbing a tree, fence or any other place above the ground. Players are allowed to hang only three times during a game. Then the player must run from *it*. The first player to be tagged with his or her feet on the ground is *it* in the next game.

Heel and Toe Race

Two teams line up to play this game as a relay race. A goal mark is chosen, such as a tree or flagpole, which is approximately 10 to 20 feet away from the players. At the signal "Go," the first player in each team races for the goal. In this race, players must set one foot forward and then place the other foot in front of it so that the heel of the front foot touches the toe of the back foot.

The racers reach the goal and return home to tag the next player on the team, who then starts out the same way. The first team to finish wins. Players who fail to touch the heel of one foot to the toe of the other foot must go back to the team and start the turn again. With a little practice, a player can scoot right along in this fun-filled race. This race is as comical to watch as it is to participate in.

Hide-and-Seek

Given the choice, kids will choose this game every chance they get. One player is *it*. One spot in the yard is *home*— such as a tree or a basketball pole. *It* stands in front of *home*, covers his or her eyes and counts by fives to 100. As soon as *it* begins counting, players run and hide. After counting to 100, *it* goes in search of the hiders. On finding a hider, *it* attempts to touch the player before he or she reaches *home*. If the hider tags *home* and shouts "ollie, ollie, otsen free" before *it* catches him or her, the hider is safe. The first hider *it* catches then becomes *it*. This is a good game to play on summer nights. (Note there are many similar versions of the hider's *home*-call.)

Home Tag

Several spots are chosen as "home" or "safety," for example, garages, sheds, or trees. The player who is chosen as *it* walks approximately 25 feet away from home as all the players stay at home. *It* then turns and says, "Anyone at home?" All the players must leave home quickly as *it* chases them to tag them. Twice during a game players may run home, where they can't be tagged. When *it* calls "Anyone at home?" any player who is at home must be *it* in the next game. Anyone *it* tags when away from home base is now *it*.

Hopscotch

Over a thousand years old, hopscotch is one of the oldest and most popular children's games of all time. There are different ways of playing, but here is one of the most common forms. A diagram such as one of those pictured on the next page is drawn with a piece of chalk on the pavement. After the players decide who goes first, second and so on, play begins.

The first player stands behind the starting line and tosses a small flat stone into box number 1. The player must hop all the way through the diagram, stop in the box containing the stone on the way back, bend over, pick up the stone and exit.

Players lose their turn if they miss the box on the toss, lose their balance, step on a line or fail to retrieve the stone properly. Otherwise, the player continues by tossing the stone into square box number 2 and goes through the same action. If a player misses a turn, he or she begins trying for the number missed on the previous turn, when it is his or her time to try again.

In the diagrams below, a player hops to box 1 on one foot, lands in 2 and 3 with both feet, hops to 4 on one foot, lands in 5 and 6 on both feet, hops to 7 on one foot, lands in 8 and 9 on both feet and then hops into 10 on one foot. Then the player turns to face the opposite direction, hopping in 10 on one foot, hops back through the rest of the boxes in the same way until reaching the box with the stone, bends over, picks up the stone and exits. The first player to make it through all the boxes on the diagram is the winner.

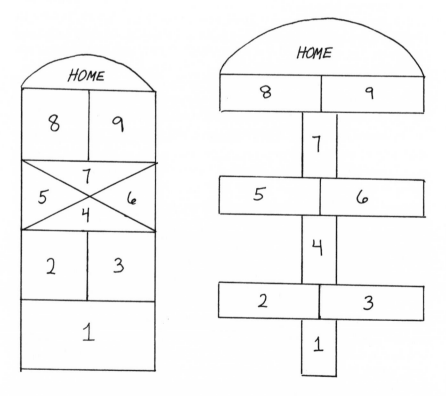

Horse

This basketball game has been delighting both children and adults for generations. A basketball goal, a basketball and at least two players are needed to play this game. When only two players are participating, the player who sinks the first free throw goes first. This player begins the game by attempting to make a basket — the more difficult the shot the better. The second player must repeat the shot identically or be assigned the letter "H," the first letter of "HORSE." Then the first player shoots again and the game continues until one player has spelled all the letters in HORSE. This player loses.

When there are three or more players, play as above. If the first player makes a basket and the second player repeats it, the third player must also make the same shot. When the second player fails in making the shot, the third player starts over, throwing in whatever style he or she wishes.

Hound and Rabbit

Players gather in groups of three, forming a little circle by putting their hands on the shoulders of the players on either side of them. They are the *hollow trees*. A *rabbit* is in the center of each threesome. An extra *rabbit* with no *hollow tree* in which to stand is present. One player is the *hound*, who chases the extra *rabbit*.

The *rabbit* runs into a *hollow tree* by ducking under the arms of the players forming the tree. The *rabbit* already in the *hollow tree* then must run to find another *hollow tree* to hide in. If *hound* tags a *rabbit* when *rabbit* is not in a *hollow tree*, *hound* becomes the *rabbit* and *rabbit* acts as the *hound* next time. If *hound* finds an empty *hollow tree*, he can go in and become a *rabbit*. Then the extra *rabbit* becomes the *hound*.

I'll Draw the Frying Pan on Your Back

This old favorite, which combines guessing and tag, always gets enthusiastic responses from young kids as well as older ones. Players stand behind *its* back. One player pretends to draw a frying pan on *its* back as the players chant:

> I'll draw the frying pan on your back.
> I'll put in some bacon.
> I'll put in some sausage.
> I'll put in some ham.
> Who will put the wiener in?

Each time an item is put in the pan, a player touches *its* back. Then *it* turns around and tries to guess who put the wiener in and assigns a penalty, for example performing 15 somersaults, doing 25 toe touches or singing a song. If *it* guesses correctly, this player completes the penalty and becomes the next *it* and the game starts over. If incorrect, *it* performs the task while the others run and hide. The game then turns into Hide and Seek. The first player caught becomes *it* for the next game.

Jacks

A game with origins dating back to ancient Greek and Roman days, Jacks is played with a set of ten small star-shaped metal pieces known as jacks and a small rubber ball. Jacks can be played alone or with two or sometimes more players on a smooth surface such as a school yard, sidewalk, table or uncarpeted floor. Each player must take a turn accomplishing a series of different feats.

There are lots of variations, but winning normally involves picking up all the jacks, one at a time, while bouncing the ball in between. When a player misses, he or she must start at that point when his or her turn comes up again. Misses include failing to catch the ball on the right bounce, not catching the ball at all, touching any jack except the ones to be picked up, failing to hold the ball or the number of jacks that have been picked up or changing the playing position. (The game must be played from the point that the player tossed the jacks.) The first player to finish all the tasks decided on in the beginning wins. Following are several variations of jacks.

BABIES

With a single toss of the right hand, the first player flings all the jacks on a smooth surface, tosses the ball up with the right hand, picks up one jack and after the ball bounces once, catches the ball in the right hand. Then the player puts this jack in the left hand and picks up all the other jacks, one by one, in the same manner.

TWOS, THREES, FOURS, FIVES, ETC.

This is played the same as Babies but the player must pick up two jacks at a time until all the jacks are gone. If the number is uneven, the player picks up the remaining single jack on the last throw. Then he or she picks up three jacks until they are all gone, then four, then five, etc., until reaching the highest number of jacks being played.

EGGS IN A BASKET

This is played the same as Babies except the jack or jacks must be placed in the left hand instead of being held in the right hand before the ball is caught.

Jump Rope

A traditional activity dating back centuries, Jump Rope was once used for answering all sorts of questions and telling fortunes as is quite apparent in the rhymes: "How many times? How many days?" One player or more is needed.

ONE JUMPER

Player holds a rope end in each hand, making sure the rope is long enough to be pulled easily over his or her head but not long enough to drag on the ground once it's turned. Player may either skip along, moving forward or backward, or stay in one spot and jump.

TWO JUMPERS

One player holds each end of the rope and the other player stands either in front or back of the first and they jump together.

THREE OR MORE JUMPERS

Two players, each holding one end of the rope, face each other and swing the rope in a circular motion above their heads. They should stand far enough apart so that the rope can be swung smoothly, barely touching the ground as it goes around with enough room in the middle for a player/players to jump.

INSTRUCTIONS

One method is to have all the players line up and take turns jumping over the rope when it is turned. Jumping can be a simple skip, a hop, a two-footed jump or whatever pattern the jumper chooses. A player may continue to jump as long as he or she wants to. If the jumper decides to quit jumping, that jumper goes to the end of the line and waits for the next turn. If the jumper continues and misses a jump or trips, he or she becomes a turner. The turner that the player replaces then gets a chance to take a turn jumping.

FOLLOW THE JUMPER

The first player completes a feat, and the other players must do exactly as the leader. If the next player completes the task, he or she may assign another one. If this player fails to repeat the action/s, that player then replaces one of the turners, who then can participate as a jumper.

RHYMES

To add to the delight of Jump Rope, players often simply chant a rhyme while jumping and counting the number of jumps or imitate actions in the rhyme. Here are a few examples:

1. Cinderella, dressed in yellow,
   Went upstairs to kiss a fellow;
   By mistake, she kissed a snake.
   How many doctors did it take?
   One, two, three four...

2. Teddy bear, Teddy bear, turn around.
   Teddy bear, Teddy bear, touch the ground.
   Teddy bear, Teddy bear tie your shoe.
   Teddy bear, Teddy bear, that will do.
   Teddy bear, Teddy bear go upstairs,
   Teddy bear, Teddy bear say your prayers.
   Teddy bear, Teddy bear, dim the light.
   Teddy bear, Teddy bear, say goodnight.

3. Down in the valley where the green grass grows
   There sits [jumper's name] as sweet as a rose.
   Along came _____[name of someone player likes]
      and kisses him/her on the cheek.
   How many kisses did she/he get? [Player
      continues jumping until he or she misses.]

4. Miss Lucy had a baby
   She named him Tiny Tim
   She put him in the bathtub
   To teach him how to swim

   He drank all the water
   He ate all the soap
   He tried to eat the bathtub
   But it wouldn't fit down his throat

   Miss Lucy called the doctor
   Miss Lucy called the nurse
   Miss Lucy called the lady
   with the alligator purse

   In came the doctor
   In came the nurse
   In came the lady
   with the alligator purse

"Mumps," said the doctor
"Measles," said the nurse
"Nothing," said the lady
with the alligator purse

Out walked the doctor
Out walked the nurse
Out walked the lady
with the alligator purse

Out came the water
Out came the soap
Out came the bathtub
that wouldn't fit down his throat.

5. I asked my mother for fifteen cents,
   To see a cow jump over the fence,
   He jumped so high
   Till he reached the sky
   He never came back till the fourth of July.
   [The players must jump higher and higher
      after the rhyme.]

6. Buster Brown, turn around,
   Buster Brown, touch the ground,
   Buster Brown, show your shoe,
   Buster Brown, You'd better skidoo.
   [Jumper must follow the instructions of the
      rhyme while jumping.]

7. First-grade babies;
   Second-grade tots;
   Third-grade angels;
   Fourth-grade snots;
   Fifth-grade peaches;
   Sixth-grade plums;
   Seventh-grade hobos;
   Eighth-grade bums.

8. I went downtown to see Miss Brown.
   She gave me a nickel to buy a pickle.
   The pickle was sour so I bought a flower.
   The flower was dead so I bought some thread.
   The thread was thin so I bought a pin.
   The pin was sharp so I bought a harp.
   And on that harp I played:
   Little Spanish dancer, give a high kick.
   Little Spanish dancer, give a high kick.
   Little Spanish dancer turn around.
   Little Spanish dancer, touch the ground.
   Spanish dancer, do the splits.
   Spanish dancer, give a high kick.
   Spanish dancer, take a sip of wine.
   Close your eyes, and count to nine —1,2,3...

Kick the Can

No matter what age, boys and girls love this exciting hiding game in which all players help to fight the one chosen to be *it*. Guarding a tin can placed inside a small circle marked on the ground, *it* counts to 100 while players hide. Trying to spy on others, *it* gradually moves away from the tin, cautiously extending his or her area of inquiry. On spotting a hider, *it* calls out the hider's name and taps on the tin three times, "One, two, three, for Cristy Sue Clodhopper." *It* tags Cristy Sue and she must come and wait by the base where the tin can is. Then *it* continues to search for other players.

Meanwhile, other hiders peep from their hideaways, trying to find a good time to rush in and kick the tin can out of the ring. Whenever this happens, all of those already caught are then free to run and hide while *it* runs to replace the can inside the circle. *It* must call in and tag all players before his or her turn ends. The last player caught is the next *it*.

King

The player chosen as *king* stands in the center with a beachball or rubber playground ball while the other players stand in the outside circle. *King* throws the ball to each player in turn, and they catch it. Next *king* throws it to each player with his or her right hand and they must catch it in their right hands and throw it back. *King* repeats this routine, throwing with the left hand, and players must do the same. If any player misses, he or she is out of the game. The game gets more difficult as play continues. *King* may invent any number of plays. The player who stays in the circle longest wins and is the next *king*.

King of the Mountain

This old favorite is best suited to youngsters six years of age and older. It's loads of fun to play in the snow. It also can be played in the summer, but a high mound is needed. One player, designated *king*, bounds to the top of the snowpile or mound and cries, "King of the Mountain." At this signal, all the other children race from a starting point approximately 20 feet away. The first one to reach the mound may run up and try to push the *king* off and become the new *king*; at this point the game begins all over again. If the *king* shoves the player off, the race starts over and the next child who reaches the mound first may try to push the *king* off and become *king* of the mountain.

Leapfrog

An all-time favorite, this outside game may be played by just two players, in which case there is no goal or winner. One player bends down, and the other vaults over that bended player's back, runs forward a few steps and bends over, making a back for the first player to leap over. It's most fun when played with a large number of kids. A goal is chosen. Two or more relay teams are formed.

Players line up in a straight line, one person behind the other. The first player on each team bends down and the next in the line leaps over him or her and runs forward a few steps, bends forward and makes a back; the second in the line jumps over each of these two players, runs forward and makes a third back. Each player who follows has one more back to leap over and makes another back until everyone is stooping.

Then the player who first bent down stands up, jumps over the line of backs and makes another back at the end of that line. Then the second person who bent down gets up as soon as he or she has been jumped over and starts jumping and so on. Things become exciting if the last player in the line stands up as fast as can be after being jumped over and follows quickly after the player who jumped over him or her. Whenever every member of one relay team has reached the goal, that team is the winner.

Lemonade

This wonderful old pastime combines a game of pretending with tag. Years ago in some areas of the country it was called Trades, because the players must act out the work that people do in different occupations. Players divide into two teams and line up facing each other along chalk lines drawn approximately 50 or more feet apart. One team is called the *challengers*; the other team is the *guessers*. *Challengers* agree on an occupation they desire to imitate, such as fireman, policeman, waitress, secretary, clown, band member, etc. *Challengers* then march across the space toward the *guessers*. The *guessers* stand at their line as the following conversation takes place:

CHALLENGERS: Here we come.
GUESSERS: Where from?
CHALLENGERS: New York. [Any city can be named.]
GUESSERS: What's your name?
CHALLENGERS: Puddin Tame.
GUESSERS: What's your number.
CHALLENGERS: Cucumber.
GUESSERS: What's your trade?
CHALLENGERS: Lemonade.
GUESSERS: Go to work in the shade.

At this point, *challengers* imitate their trade in every way they can think of. *Guessers* watch closely and try to guess the trade. When the trade is guessed correctly, the *challengers* dash back to their home line with the *guessers* chasing them. The *guessers* only have to touch a *challenger* to tag him or her out of the game. *Challengers* who make it safely back to their home line think up another trade, and play resumes until every *challenger* has been caught. Then the *challengers* become the *guessers*; the original *guessers* are now the *challengers* and get a chance to pick a trade and pantomime to the new *guessers*.

Letting Out the Doves

This delightful game of chase is the most fun when a large number of players participate (12 or more). Children file into one of three lines. Players in the center line are the *owners*; to the *owners'* left is the line of *doves*, and on the *owners'* right is the line of *hawks*.

The first player in the *owners'* line clasps hands with the first *dove* and the first *hawk* in line. Suddenly, *owner* releases *dove's* hand pushing player forward. *Dove* rushes ahead, raising and lowering his or her arms as if a bird in flight. When *dove* flies a distance, *owner* releases the first *hawk*, who also runs ahead, moving arms up and down. *Hawk* must always follow *dove's* path. When *owner* thinks *dove* can return safely to the line, *owner* cups his or her hands and claps, making a hollow sound. *Dove* can't return until this signal is given.

If *dove* arrives home safely, he or she can line up at the end of the *doves'* line for another chance. If *dove* is caught by the *hawk*, he or she is out of the game. The second one in the *owners'* line then resumes play for the next game, and the original *owner* goes to the back of that line.

Lightning Bug Hunt

A wonderful old-time pastime that kids never tire of on summer evenings, Lightning Bug Hunt is a great way to introduce children to insects. All that's needed is a jar with a lid that has slits cut in the top for air and a group of kids ready for a good time. In some areas, lightning bugs are called glowworms or fireflies. At dusk, lightning bugs gleam, gliding through the evening air. The child who captures the most lightning bugs in his or her jar is the winner. In the end, the kids release their lightning bugs. Without lightning bugs, the world would be a dimmer place.

Lion in the Pit

This is an extremely good tag game that kids of all ages like. Players form a circle and hold hands with players on each side of them. One player stands in the middle of the circle and acts as the *lion*, who tries to break through the ring. The other children grip tight as *lion* attempts to break through, dodge under players' hands and, if he or she dares, jump over the players' hands.

Players raise and lower their hands when they see *lion* coming their way, trying to stop *lion* from escaping. When *lion* manages to break through, all players chase him or her. The player who catches *lion* is then *lion* in the next game.

Marbles

This centuries-old game was extremely popular even in ancient Egypt, Greece and Rome. Throughout the ages, players have used everything from nuts to smooth round stones to play this game. There are countless ways to play marbles, but the most common goal of the game is to knock opponents' marbles out of the circle. One of the simplest ways to play involves drawing a circle approximately three to four feet in diameter on a smooth, flat ground surface. Then, players decide whether the game is being played "for keeps" or "for fun." "For keeps" means that all marbles knocked out of the circle then belong to the player who shot them out. When play is "for fun," the marbles shot out of the circle remain the property of the original owner.

The game begins when each player places the same number of marbles inside the circle. The first player to take a turn shoots a larger marble, called a "shooter," from outside the circle, attempting to knock other marbles out of the circle. (Shooting is accomplished by putting the marble on the curved forefinger, bending the thumb in back of the marble and propelling it forward in a snapping movement, making sure at least one knuckle is on the ground.) If the player succeeds in shooting marble/s out, he or she continues until missing.

Then the next player takes a turn, trying to shoot marbles out of the circle. When a player knocks out other marbles and his or her "shooter" lands inside the circle, the player may pick it up and start from the outside line and shoot again. The player who shoots the most marbles out at the end of play is the winner.

Marco Polo

This water tag game is played in a swimming pool, where there are distinct and constrained boundaries. Supervising parents like this game too because they are assured that the players participating are safe when they hear the players call out. The player chosen as *it* closes his or her eyes and counts to 50 while the other players quickly and quietly swim above or below the water to different areas of the pool, getting as far away as possible without going out of the prenamed boundaries.

Then *it* paddles around, with eyes still closed, calling out "Marco." All the other players must respond, "Polo." *It* must find and tag each player. When *it* tags a player, the player must leave the pool. Then *it* calls out "Marco" again, and the others must respond, "Polo." When all of the players have been tagged, the first one tagged in the past round becomes the new *it*.

Midnight Sardines

A great inside or outside hide-and-seek game, this is one of the most popular and fun pastimes with all ages of boys and girls. One player hides while all the others shut their eyes and count to 100. Then seekers split up and search alone. If one of the seekers finds the hider, he or she slips into the hiding place as well.

Ideally, the hiding place should be somewhere that will accommodate all players, but it never is, and as other players find it, they crowd in, and a silent squeeze becomes tighter and tighter. Gradually, players still searching become aware that the other searchers are disappearing. When the last player finds the hiding place, the "sardines" heave sighs of relief as they untangle themselves from their cramped quarters.

Minuteman Run

In this fun racing game, children form a circle and hold hands. The player who is *it* stands inside the circle. *It* then walks around the circle, tapping players' joined hands slowly and saying, "Red, white and blue, out goes you." *It* does not tap each joined set of hands but does so at random. When *it* taps joined players' hands, the two players must run around the circle in opposite directions. *It* steps into one of the empty places. The player who doesn't get back into the other empty spot is then *it*.

Mother May I

This is one of the first games children play and never want to quit playing. A goal is chosen a distance from the players, who line up side by side across the yard. the player acting as *mother* stands beside the goal and tells players one by one what actions they may take to go forward, such as, "Jody-Jane Jarvis, take three giant steps." Jody-Jane must ask, "Mother, may I?" before moving forward. If a player doesn't ask permission, that player may not complete the action and must wait for his or her next turn. *Mother* may assign any sort of action, such as two baby steps, three hops, four leaps, two skips, etc. The first player who reaches the goal is the next *mother*.

Nut Race

A great relay game that works well with kids six and older, this is a good choice when a large number of children are present. Several teams of four players each line up behind a starting point. A large bowl of nuts is set on the ground in front of the first player on each team. Approximately 20 feet away, empty other bowls are lined up, one for each team. On a signal, the first player on each team dips his or her hand into the bowl of nuts positioned at the head of that team, grabs as many nuts as possible and carries them to the empty bowl. Nuts that fall to the ground cannot be picked up.

Then the first player runs back to the team, tags the second player in his or her line and that player repeats the same actions. The winning team is the one that has the most nuts in the far bowl after every member of each team has had a turn.

Pass the Ball

This game gets raves from children. All the players stand in a circle and pass a ball. *It* stands in the middle and tries to tag the person who has the ball. *It* must tag the player while that player has the ball in his or her hands. Children pass the ball quickly around the circle. When *it* comes near, they can throw it across, calling out the player's name to whom the ball is being thrown. If that player doesn't catch the ball, he or she is then *it*. Or any player who is tagged while holding the ball is the next *it*.

Pitch Pebbles

Boys and girls get a thrill seeing how close they can throw to the mark in this game. Chalk boundary lines that mark off the field are drawn across the ground about 25 feet apart. Approximately every 5 feet in a row from one end of the field to the other, an "X" is marked. Holding a small, smooth pebble, each player stands behind the boundary line that marks off one end of the field.

Players take turns trying to toss their pebble to the first "X." The player who hits nearest the mark gets one point. All players then try for the second mark, and so on. The last try involves throwing the pebble as near to the far boundary line as possible. Whichever player has the most points wins.

Poison

Kids have enjoyed playing this game on city sidewalks for many years. Players may never step on the lines that mark off the sidewalk sections. If they do, they are "poison" and out of the game. The following are the steps that each player takes in turn. Player takes two steps in the first square and two steps in the next square. On the next turn, player can step only once in a square, jumping to the next square. If a player jumps and lands beyond the sidewalk edge, he or she is out. On the last turn, player has to hop on one foot, crossing lines but never stepping on them. The last player to avoid stepping on a line is the winner.

Pom, Pom, Pullaway

For this exciting tag game, two parallel lines are drawn about 50 feet apart on a large field or playground. All the players except *it* stand behind one line at the end of the field. *It* stands in the field and calls out a player's name: "Janie Smith, Pom, Pom, Pullaway; Come away or I'll pull you away!"

The player named runs across the field, trying to reach the far line at the other side of the field before *it* tags the player. If *it* tags the player, he or she is *it* in the following turn. If *it* fails to catch the player, *it* has to call another player and try to catch him or her. The game is even more exciting if the player being chased changes course and zigzags while running for safety.

Red Light

A favorite dating back many years to the invention of the traffic light, this game is great fun with a large group. One player is chosen to be *Red Light*. This player stands about 25 yards from the other players, with his or her back turned to them. Players stand in a straight line, shoulder to shoulder, behind the player. *Red Light* closes his or her eyes, counts to ten and yells, "Green light!" Players then run at top speed toward *Red Light*. Then he or she turns around quickly and yells, "Red light!"

The instant the other players hear this command, they must stop running immediately. If *Red Light* sees any players moving when he or she turns to face them, these players must return to the starting line. The game is repeated until one players gets close enough to tap *Red Light* on the back. This player becomes the new *Red Light*.

Red Rover

A hit every time there are a large number of kids, such as at family reunions or company picnics, this super game is played with two equal teams, which face each other. Each side has a *leader*, and *leaders* agree before play begins which will call first. Players clasp hands with teammates and stand facing the opposite team, which stands approximately five feet away. The *leader* designated to go first calls: "Red Rover, Red Rover, Send [player from the other side] Sammy Bob Swartzentrooper over."

Sammy Bob leaves his team and runs forward to the opposing team, attempting to break through their chain of clasped hands. He may make only one attempt to break the chain, although he may fake, pretending to run toward one end of the line and then switch course and lunge in the opposite direction to distract the players and catch them off guard. If Sammy Bob can't break through the line, he must join that side. If he succeeds in breaking through the chain, he returns to his team, which then has a chance to call someone over. Teams take turns calling someone over. This continues until there is one big line of people.

Ringolevio

This tag game has survived generations of youngsters and promises lots of excitement. Playing at night provides additional trepidation. Two teams form, with the same number of players on each side. One side is the *chasers*; the other side is the *runners*. "Home base" is chosen, which also acts as "jail" and should be large enough to house several players. A deck or front porch is a good choice for "home base" where the game begins.

Runners flee while *chasers* count to 20. Then *chasers* try to catch *runners*, who try to avoid being caught by running, zigzagging, dodging, etc. When a *chaser* catches a *runner*, he or she must hold on to the captive and say "Ringolevio." If the *runner* fails to struggle free before then, he or she is "captured" and must go to jail. The first player to capture a *runner* is then the *jailer* and remains near home base, guarding prisoners who are captured.

The *jailer* may not step foot inside the jail. If this happens, all prisoners are free. Prisoners may be released by free *runners*, who have only to rush through the jail, tag them and shout, "Ringolevio—free!" If several prisoners are in jail, they can stand with hands clasped. Free *runners* have to touch only one prisoner and they all are freed. Prisoners, as well as the one that freed them, must carefully avoid being tagged by the *jailer*. Anyone tagged by the *jailer* at this point is a prisoner again. *Chasers* win after all *runners* are captured. Then players switch roles, and the game starts over.

Rock School

Small kids love this game, which is played on steps. One child is chosen as *teacher*. The other players are the students. With a rock concealed in one hand, *teacher* stands facing the steps where all the students are seated on the first step, representing kindergarten. *Teacher* extends both closed fists in front of the first child. This player must choose which hand the rock is in. If correct, this student advances to the next step—first grade. If incorrect, the student remains on that step. Then *teacher* again conceals the rock and proceeds to the next student. The first student to reach the top step graduates and becomes the *teacher*. Players return to the first step, and the game begins again.

Run, Sheepie, Run

A tag game that youngsters have always loved can still be enjoyed today. It also provides playacting, which kids relish. One player acts as the *wolf* and stands in the middle of the yard. The children acting as the *sheep* stand on one side of the yard, and the child acting as m*other* stands next to a goal on the other side of the yard. *Mother* and sheep carry on a dialogue.

MOTHER: Sheep, sheep, come home.
SHEEP: Afraid, afraid.
MOTHER: What of?
SHEEP: The wolf.
MOTHER: Wolf is gone 'til ten tonight. Run, sheepie, run.

The first sheep runs and tries to make it to *mother* and the goal before being tagged by the *wolf*. If he or she does, the dialogue begins once more, and the next *sheep* tries to make it to *mother*. The first *sheep* to be tagged by the *wolf* is the next *wolf*. A new player then volunteers to act as *mother*.

Scavenger Hunt

This old game never fails to be the hit of the party. Each player is given a list of items to find within a certain amount of time. The group divides into teams. Players may go door to door around the neighborhood trying to locate these items. Some items may be simple to find, others should be more difficult. For example, simple items could be a comb, rubber band, rusty nail, empty aspirin bottle, Band-Aid, etc. Harder items might include a year-old calendar, penny with a certain year's date, crochet hook, specific-color marker or brush pen, etc. The first team to return with all or the largest number of items when the time limit is up wins.

Serpent

An unusual version of tag that kids like to play for hours on end, this game begins when players line up, placing their hands on the shoulders of the player in front of them. The player at the front of the line is the *head*, and the last in line is the *tail*. *Head* tries to tag *tail* while the others try to prevent it. The line must never be broken. Whenever *head* does touch *tail*, the second in line becomes *head*, and the first *head* goes to the end of the line and becomes the *tail*. This continues until everyone has had a turn as *head*.

Shadow Tag

Save this version of tag for sunny days only. Each player runs from *it*, making sure *it* doesn't tag his or her shadow. If *it* touches a shadow, the shadow's owner is *it*.

Snowball Tag

It's loads of fun playing tag in the snow with a mixed-age group. One player, *it*, must hit another player with a snowball in order to tag that player out. Two equal teams can be made up — one of *runners* and the other of *chasers*. The game is played until all the *runners* are caught. There is normally a boundary set off, and players may not go outside the boundary lines.

Spinning Bottle Tag

Kids love to play this variety of tag, where much of the excitement results from the anticipation of which player the spun bottle will end up pointing to. Players sit in a circle. The player designated as *it* stoops in the center and spins an empty bottle. A long-nosed bottle such as a catsup bottle works great. When the bottle stops spinning, the player whom the bottle is pointing to has to jump up and run after *it*, attempting to tag him or her.

It must exit on the opposite side of the circle from the chaser and run around the outside of the circle to the spot vacated before the chaser tags him or her. The chaser must always follow *its* path. If *it* is tagged before reaching the empty space in the circle, he or she remains *it* for the next turn. If *it* reaches the vacant spot before being tagged by the chaser, then the chaser becomes the new *it* in the next round.

Spoon Race

This exciting relay race is a winner with kids of all ages, especially at picnics and family outings. Several teams are formed, with at least four members each. Teams line up at a starting point. The first player in each line is given a large serving spoon. A bucket of water is placed at the head of each line. Teacups for each team are placed about 25 feet away on a level surface (raised or on the ground).

One person acts as judge and signals, "Go!" The first team member on each team scoops up as much water as the spoon will hold and heads for the teacups. The player may return for more water at any time along the way but must arrive at the team's teacup with at least some water in the spoon. Then the player runs back to the team as fast as possible, dropping the spoon in the bucket of water for the next team member. The first team to fill its teacup is the winner.

Statues

Kids love this game and don't want to stop playing it. One player acts as the *statue maker*. *Statue maker* takes a player by the wrist and twirls the player around. *Statue maker* announces what kind of statue each player will be. This could be an animal (cat, bird, goat, etc.) or a person (fireman, ballerina, bull fighter, clown, etc.). After players are swung, they assume a pose wherever they land. Players try to be as creative and imaginative as possible by posing like the statue they are supposed to be. Statues must remain perfectly still until the *statue maker* judges who is the best statue. If any player moves before this, he or she is eliminated. The best statue becomes the new *statue maker*.

Still Pond

Another great variation of blindfold tag, this game includes guessing which player the chaser has caught, which always gives kids a thrill. One blindfolded player stands in the middle of a circle of players. Ring players walk around the outside of the circle while the blindfolded player counts to ten aloud and says, "Still Pond. No more moving. I give you _____ steps." The blindfolded player can say any number of steps up to ten. Players take the number of steps in any direction and then stand still. The blindfolded player attempts to touch one of the other players. When this happens, the blindfolded player tries to guess this player's identity. If he or she guesses correctly, the player tagged becomes the blindfolded player.

Stoop Tag

Kids always enjoy this variation of tag. The player who is *it* runs after other players. The only way they can avoid being tagged is to stoop quickly on the ground. Players can squat only three times in a game. After that, when *it* is around, they must run away. The first player tagged standing or not entirely stooped is *it* in the next game.

Three-Legged Sack Race

Kids love to play this at family picnics or whenever there's a big crowd of players. Players choose a partner for this race because players run together. A goal is designated. Partners stand next to each other, step their touching legs inside a large feed sack, potato sack or heavy-duty plastic garbage bag and bend over to hold the sack up. On the signal "go," all the couples start off for the goal, and the pair to reach it first wins.

Touch-Wood Tag

The old saying "knock on wood" possibly came from the superstition that knocking on wood creates good luck or wards off evil. The same rule holds true in this exciting tag game. One player acts as *it* and chases the other children, attempting to tag them. Players can run to the nearest shrub, tree, fence or any other item that is wood and save themselves. *It* cannot tag them while they are touching wood. Players may save themselves only three times by touching wood. Thereafter, they must run from *it* or risk being tagged. The first player *it* tags is *it* in the following game.

Treasure Hunt

The book *Treasure Island* has been thrilling youngsters for decades of years, as has this exciting pastime. All that is needed is a good imagination and a group of enthusiastic kids to hunt for the treasure. Since kids of all ages love to play this game, the difficulty of the clues depends on the age of the children participating. For example, easier clues should be given to a younger-aged group. If the boys and girls playing are older, the clues would be more complicated.

All children play on one team, and normally the hunt is conducted outdoors. The players are given a clue, for example, "From where you start, take 20 steps backward." Players follow the clue, and near where they end up is another clue. Sometimes clues are attached to shrubbery or stuck inside a bottle. Each clue gives additional instructions, which direct players to the next clue and eventually to the treasure. A cigar box covered with aluminum foil makes a great treasure chest, which can be filled with make-believe treasures such as play money (both bills and coins), candy, outdated costume jewelry, etc. The excitement this game generates is worth the extra effort it takes to set it up.

Tug-of-War

One of the oldest and best-loved games over the centuries, Tug-of-War is great fun with a few players or lots of players and is particularly fun when played on the beach. A long, sturdy rope is banded directly in the middle with a knotted bandanna. The rope is laid on the ground in a straight line. A line is marked on the ground or sand precisely under the bandanna.

Two teams line up, one on either side of the line, with team members standing three to five feet apart and clasping the rope in their hands. Some-one acting as judge makes sure the bandanna is directly over the mark on the ground and gives a signal to begin pulling. The team that can pull the bandanna over to its side of the line wins.

Twenty Steps

This ancient guessing game always generates lots of enthusiasm from kids. One player, the *guesser*, is blindfolded, and the other players creep quietly away. The players may take as many or as few steps, big or small, as they wish, but no more than twenty steps.

Players must count their steps. After each player has taken his or her steps, one player calls out, "Ready!" and the *guesser* names one of the players. That player has to let the *guesser* know how many steps he or she took. The named player holds up his or her fingers, showing how many steps were taken. Another player tells the *guesser*, who then walks in the direction he or she thinks the player is, taking the exact number of steps called out. When the *guesser* thinks he or she is near the right player, the *guesser* tags the player and removes the blindfold. If *guesser* is correct in his or her guess, *guesser* and player exchange places. If wrong, the *guesser* takes another turn as *guesser*.

Wolf

This exceptionally exciting hide-and-seek/tag game guarantees lots of cheers from the players. The player who is *wolf* in this game not only tags other players but also hides while other players stand near home base. One of these players counts to 100 and then yells out, "Wolf!" *Wolf* may answer, "Not ready," and then the counter counts to 50 and calls "Wolf!" again. If *wolf* is ready, he remains silent, and all the players run to find *wolf*. Then *wolf* may run out of hiding, trying to tag another player before that player gets to home base. Whomever *wolf* tags must be *wolf* in the next round.

Zigzag Relay Race

A different type of relay race that kids always go for, this game requires two equal teams, with each player lining up about three feet behind the person in front of him or her. When a signal is given, the first player on each team runs to the right of the second player and past that player, out the left side of the line, across the third player, etc., until he or she reaches the end of the line. Then he or she circles around the last player in the line and zigzags back up the line in the same way, eventually tagging the second player in the line. The second player zigzags down the line, following the example of the first player. Players must be careful not to touch other team members while running in and out of the line, or they must start from the beginning once more. The team to have all its players zigzag through their line first wins.

Car
Games

MFA 97

Alphabet Game

A trip goes so much faster when this game is played. Each person searches independently and tries to be the first to find every letter of the alphabet on signs along the road (road signs, billboards, neon signs, etc.). Players must find the letters in alphabetical order. Whenever they find a letter from a sign, that letter should be the first letter of a word. For instance, if a sign reads, "Slippery Asphalt," a player may point it out and say, "A for asphalt."

Then the player searches for a sign displaying the letter *B* beginning a word from another sign. The first one to find every letter is the winner. If no one finds all the letters, the one who has found the most letters wins. This game becomes harder when looking for *Q*, *X* and *Z*. Things get exciting when a player finds a "Deer Xing" or "Pedestrian Xing" sign. This game is both fun and educational.

Animal, Vegetable, Mineral

This game makes a car trip go much faster. Kids and adults both like to get in on this pastime. The following definitions apply in this game: Animal — animals, birds, fish or insects; Vegetable — vegetables, plants, trees or bushes; Mineral — anything that isn't animal or vegetable and is a solid inorganic substance found in nature. One player, *it*, begins the game by telling other players what category contains the item that he or she is thinking about, for example, "I am thinking of an animal."

The rest of the players take turns asking one question, which can be answered by "yes" or "no," trying to uncover the identity of the animal. For example: "Does it have four legs?" "Does it live in the water?" "Is it an insect?" *It* keeps track of the number of questions asked. When a player guesses the right answer, he or she wins and is the next *it*. When 20 questions are asked and no correct answer has been guessed, *it* reveals the answer, and another player takes a turn as *it*.

Car Count

Boys and girls who know colors and how to count happily pass the time on a trip playing this game. Everyone names a different color. Whenever that color of car is seen, that player calls it out and keeps a count. The one who has the largest count at the end of the trip is the winner.

Ghost

Kids who like spelling games find this one challenging and lots of fun. Two or more players may participate. A dictionary comes in handy to solve any conflicts that may arise.

The first player says any letter that comes to mind. Each player in turn adds a letter. Players may end a word with three or fewer letters but may not end a word containing four or more letters. Whenever they do, they are assigned one of the letters of the word "GHOST." For example, if the first player says "e" and the second person "a," the next player may say "t" and end the word "eat." The next child must continue by adding another letter but may not end a word. A player would not add "s" because that would be a four-letter word — "eats." He or she would try to think of a longer word beginning with "eat." The person adds the fourth letter but must have a word in mind.

If a player thinks another player is bluffing, he or she may challenge that person. For instance, if the fourth player adds the letter "e," and another player challenges, player four would say, "The word I had in mind is 'eateries.' The challenging player would then have a "G" on him or her. Whenever a player has all five letters of the word "GHOST," he or she is out of the game. Play continues until all players have been eliminated except one, who is the winner.

Graveyard

Each child names a different animal — dog, cat, cow, horse, bird, sheep or pig, etc. Players call out whenever they spot their animal and keep a count of them. When a graveyard is seen, all animals are "buried." The person with the largest count wins the round, and the game begins again. Players must pick a different animal in each round.

Hangman

This fun pastime dates back many hundreds of years and can be enjoyed by two players (in which case it is a good game to play in the car) or by two teams. Each side is given a piece of paper and a pencil. Side one chooses a word of five letters or more and draws the appropriate number of dashes on a piece of paper (see drawing next page). Then side two copies the dashes onto its piece of paper. Side two tries to guess a letter of the word, and if the guess is right, that letter is written in the proper place on the line of dashes.

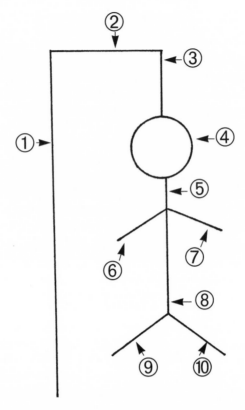

When a letter guessed appears more than once in the word, it should be written on each dash where it belongs. If the guess is incorrect, side one begins to draw the gallows for "Hangman," and the incorrect letter is recorded below the line of dashes so it won't be guessed again. Side two gets ten guesses because this is how many strokes it takes to draw the gallows and the "hangman."

Minister's Cat

Players have to think quickly in this delightful game, which is both challenging and fun. Children sit in a circle. The first player begins by slapping his or her thighs and clapping his or her hands together twice and saying, "The minister's cat is a _____ cat" naming an adjective beginning with the letter A. The next player repeats the same actions and words, naming an adjective starting with the letter B. The chant and clapping should be fast. If a player cannot think of a word in alphabetical order to describe the "minister's cat," that player is out.

Odd and Even

Although this game is known to date back over two thousand years, it still charms youngsters today. This game is played by two children. Kids stay entertained in the car for quite a while playing this one. Players look at each other while forming a fist with one of their hands. One player chooses "odd"; the other child chooses "even."

Players extend and withdraw their fists, counting together, "One, two, three, shoot!" They immediately display either their index finger or their first two fingers extended to form a *V*. When both players show the same sign, the player who chose even wins. If the players show different signs, the child who picked odd wins. Normally, players continue keeping their choice of "odd" or "even" until one player has won, say, five out of seven rounds. Then players can take the opposite choice, and play begins again. It's a simple game but, fun nonetheless.

Old Dead Horse

This is a wonderfully funny pastime that works well in the car. Lots of giggling goes on in this game, in which two or more players may participate. The quicker the pace is, the better. All players chant, "Old dead horse in the middle of the road." The first player begins, "I one it." The next person responds, "I two it."

Players continue taking turns, increasing the number each time up through the statement, "I seven it." The following player must point to the next player and say, "I jumped over it and you eight (ate) it." That player is the one that "ate the old dead horse." If the player forgets to jump over it and says, "I eight it," he or she is guilty of eating the old dead horse. The player next to the person who "eight (ate) it" starts the next round. Kids like to substitute other animals for the horse: rat, goat, opossum, skunk, etc.

Paper, Rock, Scissors

This is a fun game for two players to kill time on a long trip. With closed fists raised, they pretend to pound them as they count, "one, two, three." On the count of three, they make one of three finger formations: the palm-down flat hand is "paper"; the clenched palm-down fist is "rock"; and the two extended fingers are "scissors." If both players make the same sign, it is a tie. If they present different signs, one of them wins: paper can wrap around rock and wins over rock; rock dulls and beats scissors, and scissors cut and win over paper.

Riddly, Riddly, Riddly D

This is a good guessing game for kids who know colors. The first player says, "Riddly, riddly, riddly d, I see something that you don't see and the color is_____" and names the color of the object he or she wants the others to guess. The others take turns guessing what the object is. The item must be inside the car, if that is where the game is being played. The child who guesses correctly starts the next round.

Squaring Dots

This popular old game is a cinch to kill boredom in the car or on rainy days. Two to three players work best playing this one because of the long wait for a turn. Six to ten dots are drawn horizontally on a blank piece of paper approximately an inch apart across the page. Then six to ten rows are drawn directly underneath the first row, as follows:

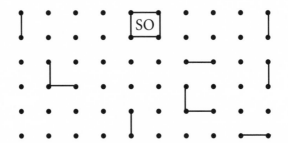

Players take turns drawing a straight line, either horizontally or vertically, connecting two dots. Slanting lines can't be drawn. The players' goal is to close a square, and when this happens, the player who closed it writes his or her initials in it and then is awarded another turn at drawing another line. The player with his or her initials in the most squares when all the squares are closed wins.

State License Plates

This is especially fun when traveling on a long trip. Pencil and paper are needed. Everyone tries to locate license plates from as many states as possible.

Each time a different state license plate is spotted, the person calling it out first gets to put it on his or her list. No other player may claim that state after that. The player identifying the most states is the winner. It's exciting to find far-away state license plates.

Tic-Tac-Toe

This is a popular game for two players and works well while traveling or any other time. It develops strategy and concentration skills. A graph is drawn such as shown. The first player chooses a box and marks it with either an *X* or an *O*. Then the second person marks another box with the opposite letter. Players alternate until one player has three boxes in a row—across, up-and-down or diagonally. This player is the winner. If neither player has accomplished this after all the boxes are filled, the old saying is "the cats win it."

Graph:	First Player	Second player

Twenty Questions

Like "Animal, Vegetable, Mineral," this is a great car game for older kids. The difference is that in this game, the players guess a famous or well-known person. That individual can be fictitious (a character from a story or a cartoon character, for example) or real. One player starts by thinking of a well-known identity and says, "Who am I?" Players must guess the right name within 20 questions, which should be answered by "yes" or "no."

The first player keeps track of the number of questions. Players should find out within the first few questions if the person is real or fictitious, an entertainer, politician, in public life, or whatever. If the group fails to answer correctly within 20 questions, the player gets another chance to pick another character for the group to identify. If the group guesses the identity within 20 questions, the player who makes the right guess then has a chance to ask, "Who am I?"

Card
Games

MFA 97

Authors

Kids have a good time playing this card game, which is more exciting when four to six players participate. A special deck of cards showing famous authors and the titles of four of their books may be used. Authors may also be played with a standard deck of cards. Using a standard card deck, the ranks of the cards become the "author," and the suits are the "books." For example, a player holding the ten of diamonds, spades, and hearts would ask for the ten of clubs to complete his or her "book" of tens. Each player tries to get as many complete "book" collections as possible.

The dealer deals out all the cards. It doesn't matter if some players have one more card than the others. Players look at their cards and sort them into groups. The player on the dealer's left asks any player by name for a particular card. The player must already have at least one of the same rank, that is, if a player asks for a four of diamonds, he or she must be holding a four of some other suit.

If the person asked has the card, it is given to the player asking for it. The asking player may again ask anybody for a card as long as he or she already has one card of that rank. The player continues until he or she fails to receive a requested card. If the person asked doesn't have the card asked for, it is then that player's turn to ask for cards.

Whenever a player collects all four cards of the same rank, he or she immediately shows it and places it in a face-down pile in front of him or her. The person collecting the most "books" at the end is the winner.

Beggar My Neighbor

Here's a simple and exciting game in which kids don't have to pay too much attention to have a great time. There may be two to six players. A standard deck is used. If more than three children play, two decks may be mixed. The dealer deals out all cards one at a time, face down. Some players may have one card more than the others. Players do not look at their cards and put them in a face-down pile in front of them.

Beginning with the player on the dealer's left, players take turns putting the top card from their piles face up in a pile in the center of the table. When an ace, king, queen, or jack is played, the next player in turn must turn over a certain number of cards from his or her pile, placing them on the central pile — four cards for an ace, three cards for a king, two cards for a queen and one card for a jack.

After payment is made, the entire pile becomes the property of the player who played the ace, king, queen or jack and is placed face down at the bottom of his or her own pile. If one of the payment cards is an ace, king, queen, or jack, the payer stops turning over cards and the next player has to pay the correct number of cards.

This continues until a player paying out cards turns over the correct number of cards containing no aces, kings, queens or jacks. Then the last player to have turned over an ace or face card may take the central pile and place it face down at the bottom of his or her own pile. The payer starts a new round, playing his or her next card face up in the center. The winner is the person with all the cards in the end.

Crazy Eights

One of the most popular card games, Crazy Eights can be played by two to four players. A standard card deck is used. With two players, seven cards are dealt. When three or four players play, five cards are dealt. The rest of the cards form the stock and are placed face down on the table with the top card turned up to form the "starter" pile. If the first card turned up is an eight, it is buried and the next card in the stock is turned up.

The player to the dealer's left starts by putting on the top of the middle pile any card of the same suit, any card with the same point value or any eight (this is a wild card.) For example, if the starter card is a queen of diamonds, any diamond, any queen or any eight may be played on it. The object of the game is to be rid of all cards.

When a player throws a card with the same value as the face up card but of a different suit, the suit is automatically changed. The player throwing an eight may change the suit to any of the other suits by saying, "This is a heart (spade, diamond or club)." The next player must throw a card of the called suit or another eight. If that player throws an eight on top of another eight, he or she may change the suit. Eights act as wild cards to change suit but not rank. The value remains eight. If a player can't make a play, he or she must draw cards from the top of the stock and add them to his or her hand until able to play.

When the stock is exhausted, the person unable to play must pass and miss a turn. The following player then takes a turn. Players may draw from the stock even if they have a playable card. Normally, stock is not gone before the game ends, but not always. The winner is the player who gets rid of all his or her cards.

Donkey

In this fast and noisy game of hilarity, players are penalized with letters from the game's name. "Donkey" is usually played with sets of cards taken from a deck of standard playing cards. Each card set consists of four cards with the same picture or number. For instance, if four players are playing, the aces, kings, queens and jacks only could be used. If seven players participate, cards ace through seven might be used, discarding all higher cards. It doesn't matter what ranks are chosen.

In the beginning, any unbreakable objects such as spoons or pencils are placed in the center of the table. There should be one less object than the number of players. Youngsters try to collect a set of four cards while they try to avoid becoming the "donkey." The dealer deals out all chosen cards. Players choose one card they do not want and pass it to the player to their left. Players look at their new cards and again choose a card to pass. They may pass the new card passed to them if they wish.

The game continues in this way as quickly as possible until one player has a set of four cards of the same kind. This player should quietly put the set face up on the table and pick up an object from the center of the table. The player who doesn't pick up an object loses the round and is penalized with a letter of the word "donkey." The player penalized with all letters of the word "donkey" must he-haw three times.

Fish

This is one of the most popular of all children's card games and one of the first that kids learn to play. Fish is a game for two people or more — the more the better. A standard card deck is used. Cards are dealt one by one. With two players, seven cards are dealt; if more players participate, they receive five cards. The rest of the pack is placed face down in the center of the table to become the stock.

Players sort the cards in their hands. In the beginning, the person left of the dealer asks any player by name for a card of a specific rank: "Clancy, give me your aces." The player asking must have another ace in his or her hand. The player asked must surrender any aces. The asker's turn continues so long as he or she succeeds. If the player asked doesn't have any cards of that rank, he or she says, "Go fish." The asking player then draws from the fish pile.

Play continues with the player who said "go fish" asking for cards. When a player gets a *book* (four cards of the same rank), he or she shows them and puts them in front of himself or herself. The first player to have no cards in his or her hand wins. If two players finish at the same time, the one with the most completed sets wins.

I Doubt It

This is a fun game for risk-takers and those who like calling others' bluffs. At least three players are needed, but the more the better. Either one or two standard decks are used. The dealer deals out all the cards. Some players may have an extra card. Players try to be the first to get rid of all their cards.

After players look at their cards, the player holding the two of clubs says how many two cards he or she is placing face down in a pile in the center. The player may actually place more cards than claimed to get rid of cards. In turn, following players must then play or claim they are playing one to four cards of the rank one higher than those played by the last player.

Whenever a player thinks another is cheating, player calls out, "I doubt it." The challenged player has to turn over the cards played for inspection. If the doubting player is right, the cheating player must pick up all the cards in the central pile and add them to his or her hand. If the player didn't cheat, the doubting player has to take the central pile and starts the next round beginning with the next number in sequence.

Memory

A great game for any number of players, this game is easy to play. It is an excellent test of memory and helps children recognize numbers. One or two decks of standard playing cards are used, depending on the number of players. The playing area should be large and flat — the floor is the best choice.

In the beginning, the player choosing the highest card from the deck is the dealer. After shuffling the cards, the dealer lays them face down on the floor in all directions. No card should touch another card. Players try to collect as many cards as possible by turning up pairs. The player to the left of the dealer begins by turning over two cards at random, allowing the other players to see them. If they are a match — for example, two nines, or two aces — the player takes them and may turn over two more cards until he or she has a mismatch.

The player to the dealer's left then turns over a card. If it is a card that matches one that has already been turned over, the player must try to remember where that card is. He or she turns over a second card and tries to get a match. If successful, the player takes the pair. If no match is made, play continues with players taking their turns in a clockwise direction until all cards have been collected. The player with the most cards at the end of the game wins.

My Ship Sails

This is an easy beginners' game and is also exciting when played at a fast pace by players familiar with the game. Four to seven people may play. A standard deck of cards is used. Players aim to be the first to collect seven cards of the same suit. The player drawing the highest card from the deck deals the cards in a clockwise direction — one at a time and face down until each player has seven cards. The rest of the cards aren't used.

Players sort their cards into suits and decide which suit to collect. This is normally the suit for which they have the most cards. They may change their minds later in the game and choose another suit. Players take one card they don't want and put it face down on the table. When all the players are ready, they pass these cards to the person to their right. Players pick up their new card, discard another card and pass it to the right. Play continues until one person collects seven cards of the same suit and calls, "My ship sails." This player is the winner.

Old Maid

Old Maid is a great favorite with young children. A special Old Maid deck or a standard card deck can be used. The Old Maid card deck has a single card with a picture of the "old maid" and pairs of cards with other funny characters. When using standard playing cards, three queens are removed, leaving the deck with an odd queen — the "old maid." This game is for three or more players.

The dealer deals all cards face down, one at a time, to the players. Some players may end up with one card more than the others. Players try to get rid of all their cards by discarding cards of equal value. Players look at their cards, searching for any matching character cards or playing cards with the same value — two fives or two jacks — and laying them face down on the table. If players have three cards of the same value, they may put down only two and must keep the third. If they have four cards of the same value, they may put down all four as two pairs.

The person left of the dealer fans out his or her cards, offering them to the player on the left. This player picks a card and looks to see if the card drawn matches up with any of the cards he or she is holding. If a match is found, it is laid face down on the table. If not, the new card is added to the player's hand. The game continues until all cards but the "old maid" have been played. The player holding the "old maid" card at the end loses. No one wins this game.

Seven Up

Also known as Fan-Tan, this game dates back hundreds of years and still remains a favorite with kids today. Three to five players may play. The dealer deals out all cards, one at a time, face down to the players. The cards don't always come out evenly. The player to the dealer's left starts by placing any seven face up in the middle of the table. If that player has no seven, the next player on the left searches his or her hand for a seven.

The game continues with each player taking a turn. Players have several options: (1) place a seven in the middle of the table to form a seven pile; (2) build up on one of the sevens in the middle by playing a card one rank higher but of the same suit on a seven pile; (3) build down on one of the sevens in the middle by throwing a card one rank lower but of the same suit on a seven pile; (4) pass when they cannot throw a seven or build up or down on a seven pile.

Play goes on until one of the players gets rid of all of his or her cards. This player is the winner of the round. Then the others count the cards left in their own hands. The winner of this round scores the total number of cards held by the other players. Say there are three other players — one player holding four cards, one with three cards and the other with two cards. The winner of the round would have a total score of nine. Scores are recorded on a sheet of paper. The dealer of the next round is the player to the left of the first dealer. The first player to score 100 points is the winner.

Slap Jack

Two or more players can play this game. The only skill that players need for this exciting game is to be able to recognize a jack. Players aim to win all the cards. Standard playing cards are used. If there are more than three players, two decks can be mixed. The dealer deals out all the cards in a clockwise direction. It doesn't matter if some players have one card more than the others. Players may not look at their cards. The player to the dealer's left turns over the top card on his or her pile, placing it face up in the center.

Play continues with each player placing a card on the top on the previous player's card. When a jack is turned up, each player attempts to "slap the jack." If more than one person slaps the jack, the person whose hand is underneath wins the pile. The next player then starts another round, placing a card face up in the center. If players slap a card that isn't a jack, they must give their top card to the player whose card was slapped in error. The winner is the person who collects all the cards.

Snap

This noisy and fun game is one of the greatest-loved children's card games. Two or more can play. A standard deck is used. It doesn't matter if any cards are missing. It's a good idea to use two decks if more than three people are playing. Players strive to win all the cards. The dealer deals out all cards in a clockwise direction — face down, one at a time. It's OK if some players have more cards than the others.

Players put cards in a neat face-down pile in front of them. Players may not look at their cards. The player to the dealer's left turns over the top card of his or her face-down pile and places it face up to start a face-up pile of cards next to his or her face-down pile. The player to the left does the same and so on around the players. Whenever any player sees that the top cards of any two face-up piles have the same value — two kings, two sixes, two tens, etc.— that player shouts, "Snap!" This player collects both piles of cards and places them at the bottom of own face-down pile.

Play continues with the player to the left of the last player who turned over a card. If two players shout "snap!" together, the matching face-up piles are pooled in the center. Players continue turning over cards. The first player to shout "snap pool!" when the top card of any player's face-up pile matches the top pool card collects the pool pile along with the face-up pile and places them at the bottom of his or her own face-down pile.

Whenever players run out of face-down cards, they turn over their face-up cards on their next turn. If a player calls "snap!" in error, that player must give one card from his or her own face-down pile to each of the other players. The winner is the player with all the cards in the end.

War

War is an easy game that kids always enjoy. It's a good way of introducing children to card playing. It is a game for two. Use a complete deck of standard playing cards. Players try to win all the cards. The dealer deals all the cards. Players put their cards face down in a neat pile in front of them. Without looking at the cards, both players turn over the top card of their piles and place them face up, side by side, in the center. Whoever has the higher card, regardless of suit, wins both cards and places them face down at the bottom of his or her pile.

The highest cards are aces, followed by kings, queens, jacks and so on down from the tens to the twos. When the two cards turned up have the same value, war is on. Players put one card face down on top of their first card in the center. Then they put another card face up on top of it. These two new face-up cards are compared, and the higher card wins all six cards in the center. If the new face-up cards match, war continues until someone plays a card higher than the other. The winner is the player to win all the cards or the player who has the most cards at the end of a time limit set before the start of the game.

Singing Games and Campfire Songs

MFA 97

A-Hunting We Will Go

ACTIONS

For this old-time favorite singing game, two groups of children line up facing each other. During the first two lines of the song, the *head couple* join crossed hands, skipping down the center to the foot of the line. All players sing and clap hands to the rhythm.

On the third and fourth lines, the *head couple* skip back to the head of the line. The song is repeated as the two members of the *head couple* drop hands and skip around the outside of their own lines to the foot of the line, followed by players in their line. When the *head couple* meet at the foot, they join hands to form an arch, and other players skip with partners under the arch. The *head couple* stays at the foot of the line. The second couple becomes the new *head couple*.

SONG

Billy Boy

This song is fun when the girls sing the question lines and the boys answer Billy's lines.

Oh— where have you been, Bil-ly Boy, Bil-ly
Boy? Oh— where have you been, charming Bil-ly?
I have been to seek a wife; She's the joy— of my
life; She's a young thing and can-not leave her moth-er —

Can she bake a cherry pie, Billy Boy, Billy Boy?
Can she bake a cherry pie, charming Billy?
She can bake a cherry pie,
Quick as a cat can wink an eye,
But she's a young thing and cannot leave her mother.

Bingo

This wonderfully funny old song's chorus is great for "clapping rhythm."

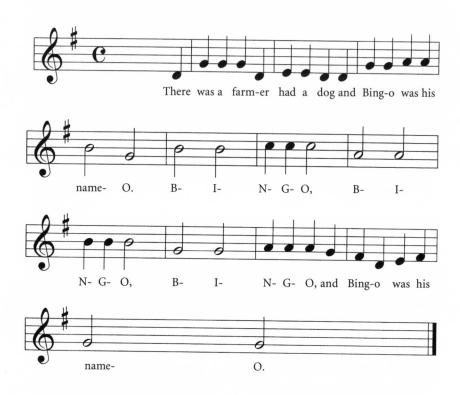

There was a farm-er had a dog and Bing-o was his name- O. B- I- N- G- O, B- I- N- G- O, B- I- N- G- O, and Bing-o was his name- O.

2. (Repeat first and second lines.)
   B-I-N-G (one clap)
   B-I-N-G (one clap)
   B-I-N-G (one clap)
   And Bingo was his name O.

3. (Repeat first and second lines.)
   B-I-N (two claps)
   B-I-N (two claps)
   B-I-N (two claps)
   And Bingo was his name O.

4. (Repeat first and second lines.)
   B-I (three claps)
   B-I (three claps)
   B-I (three claps)
   And Bingo was his name O.

5. (Repeat first and second lines.)
   B (four claps)
   B (four claps)
   B (four claps)
   And Bingo was his name O.

6. (Repeat first and second lines.)
   Five claps
   Five claps
   Five claps
   And Bingo was his name O.

Blue-Tail Fly

When I was young, I used to wait, up-
on old mast-er and pass his plate; and pass the bot- tle when
he got dry, and brush a- way the blue- tail fly.

CHORUS

Jim-my crack corn and I don't care; Jim-my crack corn and
I don't care; Jim-my crack corn and I don't care; My
mast- er's gone a- way.

2. One day he rode around the farm;
   The flies so numerous, they did swarm;
   One chanced to bite him on the thigh;
   The devil take the blue-tail fly.
   (**chorus**)

3. And when he'd ride in the afternoon,
   I'd follow with a hickory broom;
   The pony being very shy,
   Got bitten by the blue-tail fly.
   (**chorus**)

4. The pony run, he jump, he pitch;
   He threw old master in a ditch;
   He died, the jury wondered why;
   The verdict was the blue-tail fly.
   (**chorus**)

5. They laid him under a 'simmon tree;
   His epitaph is there to see;
   "Beneath the stone I'm forced to lie,
   A victim of the blue-tail fly."
   (**chorus**)

Clapping Rhythm

Children have enjoyed clapping rhythms for over a century. It creates added fun when children are singing songs. Two children face each other and clap, keeping rhythm to the song. Here is one variety of "clapping rhythm." The following actions are repeated over and over until the song ends: Slap own thighs, own hands together, right hands slap, own hands together, left hands slap, own hands together, opened hands slap, own hands together.

Did You Ever See a Lassie?

ACTIONS

This cute singing game is so old that it dates back to a time when girls and young women were called "lassie." Kids still enjoy it with as much enthusiasm today. Players circle around, singing. Each time they come to "This way and that way," they stop going around and act out an appropriate action for whatever character is named, for example, lassie, baker, painter, fireman, clown, etc. Before the song begins, the children decide what people will be imitated.

SONG

[The children prance around like dressed up ladies, powdering their faces or putting on lipstick.]

  2. Did you ever see a baker, a baker, a baker,...

[The children pretend to roll dough, cut doughnuts and put things in an oven.]

Down in the Valley

2. Roses love sunshine, violets love dew;
   Angels in heaven, know I love you.
   Know I love you dear, know I love you;
   Angels in heaven, know I love you.

3. Write me a letter, send it by mail;
   Send it in care of the Birmingham jail.

The Birmingham jail dear, the Birmingham jail;
Send it in care of the Birmingham jail.

4. Build me a castle forty feet high;
   So I may see him as he goes by.
   As he goes by dear, as he goes by;
   So I may see him as he goes by.

Farmer in the Dell

ACTIONS

The children stand in a circle and act out this song as they sing. The player who is *farmer* stands in the middle. As each player is chosen, he or she joins the *farmer*. The *farmer* takes one from the circle for his wife; she takes one for a child; and so on. When the rat takes the *cheese*, the *cheese* joins the others in the middle.

On the verse "The cheese stands alone," the *cheese* moves outside the circle until the verse is finished. Then the *rat* chases the *cheese*. If the *cheese* can circle around and make it back to the group before being caught, the *cheese* is safe and the game continues, with the *rat* taking the part of the *farmer*. If the *rat* catches the *cheese*, the *cheese* is the *farmer* and the game proceeds.

SONG

2. The farmer takes a wife,
   The farmer takes a wife,
   Heigh-o, the merry-o,
   The farmer takes a wife.

There are six additional verses, following the same format as verse one and two:

3. The wife takes a child,

4. The child takes a nurse,

5. The nurse takes a cat,

6. The cat takes a rat,

7. The rat takes the cheese,

8. The cheese stands alone,

Found a Peanut

Kids get lots of laughs from this song.

Found a pea- nut; Found a pea- nut; Found a

pea- nut, ju- st now. Ju- st now I found a

pea- nut, Found a pea- nut, ju- st now.

2. It was rotten; (Repeat as in first verse)

3. Ate it anyway; (etc.)

4. Got sick; (etc.)

5. Called the doctor; (etc.)

6. I died; (etc.)

7. Went to heaven; (etc.)

8. Got reborn; (etc.)

9. Found a peanut; (etc.)

Froggie Went A-Courtin'

Frog-gie went a-court-in' and he did ride, mm- hmm (mm-

hmm). Frog-gie went a-court-in' and he did ride, mm-

hmm (mm- hmm). Frog-gie went a-court-in' and

he did ride, Sword and pis- tol by his side, mm-

hmm, mm- hmm (mm- hmm)!

2. Rode up to Miss Mousey's door, ho-
   ho (ho-ho).
   Rode up to Miss Mousey's door, ho-
   ho (ho-ho).
   Rode up to Miss Mousey's door,
   Where he'd often been before, ho-ho,
   ho-ho (ho-ho)!

3. Said, Miss Mousey are you within,
   ah-hah? (ah-hah)?
        (Repeat twice more as before.)
   Yes kind sir, I sit and spin, tee-hee,
   tee-hee (tee-hee)!

4. Took Miss Mousey on his knee, mm-
   hmm (mm-hmm).
   Said, Miss Mousey will you marry
   me? Please do. Please do.
   (Please do!)

5. Why, without my Uncle Rat's con-
   sent, oh no (oh no).
   I wouldn't marry the president,
   oh no, oh no (oh no)!

6. Uncle Rat laughed till he shook his fat sides,
   ha-ha (ha-ha).
   To think that his niece would be a
   bride, ha-ha, ha-ha (ha-ha)!

7. Where shall the wedding supper be,
   mm-hmm (mm-hmm).
   Down in the swamp in the holler
   'simmon tree, mm-hmm,
   mm-hmm (mm-hmm)!

8. What shall the wedding supper be?
   yum-yum (yum-yum)!
   Fried mosquito and black-eyed peas,
   yum-yum, yum-yum (yum-yum)!

9. First to come in a mealey moth,
   mm-hmm (mm-hmm).
   And she laid out the table cloth, ah-
   hah, ah-hah (ah-hah)!

10. Next to come in was a doodley bug,
    mm-hmm (mm-hmm).
    And he was totin' that little brown
    jug, glub-glub, glub-glub (glub-glub)!

11. Next to come in was a bumberly
    bee, b-zzz (b-zzz).
    With a big bass fiddle on his knee,
    b-zzz, b-zzz (b-zzz)!

12. Next to come in was a cumberly
    cow, moo-oo (moo-oo).
    Tried to dance but she didn't know
    how, moo-oo, moo-oo (moo-oo)!

13. Cornbread and clabber milk settin'
    on the shelf, mm-hmm (mm-hmm).
    If you want any more you can sing it
    for yourself, that's all, that's all
    (that's all)!

Git Along Little Dogies

To make more room for the music on page 70, verse 2 is run here.

2. Early in spring we round up the dogies,
   We mark 'em and brand 'em and bob
   off their tails;
   Round up the horses, load up the
   chuck wagon,

Then throw the dogies out on the
long trail.
(repeat chorus.)

Here We Go Looby Loo

ACTIONS

In the following old-time favorite, children stand in a circle and act out the words. For example, in the first verse, all the kids put their right hands forward to the center of the circle and then turn around. Then the same is done with the left hand, right foot, left foot and then whole self. During the chorus, the kids hold hands and promenade in a circle.

SONG

2. I put my left hand in (etc.)
   (Repeat chorus.)

3. I put my right foot in (etc.)
   (Repeat chorus.)

4. I put my left foot in (etc.)
   (Repeat chorus.)

5. I put my whole self in (etc.)
   (Repeat chorus.)

Here We Go Round the Mulberry Bush

ACTIONS

Young boys and girls have delighted in this, one of the most famous of all children's singing games, for hundreds of years. It originated as a marriage song and dance. Guests sang and danced around a bush they considered sacred. Children form a ring, join hands and move in a circle while singing the chorus. Then they stand still, release hands and perform the action in the next verse.

SONG

1. This is the way we wash our clothes,
   We wash our clothes, we wash our clothes,
   This is the way we wash our clothes
   So early Monday morning.

2. This is the way we iron our clothes,
   (repeat as in verse 1)
   So early Tuesday morning.
   (chorus)

3. This is the way we sweep our floor (etc.)
   So early Wednesday morning.
   (chorus)

4. This is the way we scrub our floor (etc.)
   So early Thursday morning.
   (chorus)

5. This is the way we bake our bread (etc.)
   So early Friday morning.
   (chorus)

6. This is the way we run and play (etc.)
   So early Saturday morning.
   (chorus)

7. This is the way pray at church (etc.)
   So early Sunday morning.
   (chorus)

Home on the Range

Oh   give   me   a   home, where the buf- fa-   lo

roam,   where the   deer   and the   an-   te-   lope   play;

Where   sel-   dom   is   heard   a   dis-   cour- ag-   ing

word,   And the   skies   are   not   cloud-y   all   day.

CHORUS

Home,   home   on   the   range,

Where the   deer   and the   an-   te-   lope   play;

Where   sel-   dom   is   heard   a   dis-   cour- ag-   ing

word,   And the skies   are   not   cloud- y   all   day.

Hush, Little Baby

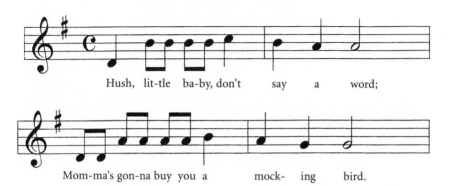

Hush, lit-tle ba-by, don't say a word;

Mom-ma's gon-na buy you a mock- ing bird.

2. If that mockingbird don't sing,
   Momma's gonna buy you a diamond ring.

3. If that diamond ring gets broke,
   Momma's gonna buy you a billy goat.

4. If that billy goat don't pull,
   Momma's gonna buy you a cart 'n' bull.

5. If that cart 'n' bull turn over,
   Momma's gonna buy you a dog named Rover.

6. If that dog named Rover won't bark,
   Momma's gonna buy you a horse 'n' cart.

7. If that horse 'n' cart fall down,
   You'll still be the sweetest little baby in town.

I Am a Funny Little Dutch Girl

Girls find this a wonderful and funny song to sing with "clap rhythm."

My boyfriend came from England;
My boyfriend came from France,
My boyfriend came from the USA
And boy how he can dance.

My boyfriend gave me peaches;
My boyfriend gave me pears,

My boyfriend gave me 15 cents
And kissed me on the stairs.

I gave him back his peaches;
I gave him back his pears;
I gave him back his 15 cents,
And kicked him down the stairs.

I'm a Nut

I'm an a- corn, small and round, ly- ing on the

cold, cold ground. Peo- ple come and step on me;

that's why I'm so cracked, you see. I'm a nut (tsk! tsk!) I'm a

nut (tsk! tsk!) I'm a nut (tsk! tsk!) I'm a nut.

2. I'm so nutty, I don't know
   why the squirrels love me so.
   I'm descended from an oak;
   Nuts to you and that's no joke.
   I'm a nut (tsk! tsk!)
   I'm a nut (tsk! tsk!)
   I'm a nut (tsk! tsk!)
   I'm a nut.

In and Out the Windows

ACTIONS

This popular singing game is a crowd-pleaser every time. All players except one form a circle, link hands, hold their arms high, making arches, and sing the song as *middle player* runs in and out under their arms. On the line "As we have done before," *middle player* chooses one from the circle. *Chosen player* leads off holding hands with *middle player* and everyone sings next verse. These two continue to run in and out under other players' arms until the verse ends.

Then the second *chosen player* picks a third player in the same way to run with them and the thirds picks a fourth, etc. Children continue singing, repeating from verse one if necessary, and the game proceeds until finally there are no players left in the circle. They are winding around in serpentine fashion behind the player who was *middle player*.

SONG

2. Round and round the village,
   Round and round the village,
   Round and round the village,
   As we have done before.

3. Go and face your lover,
   Go and face your lover,

   Go and face your lover,
   As you have done before.

4. Follow her to London,
   Follow her to London,
   Follow her to London,
   As we have done before.

Itsy Bitsy Spider

ACTIONS

First line: Children sit in a circle. Touching the pointer finger of the right hand to the thumb of the left hand, they pivot them, placing the right thumb to the left index finger and walking their fingers over their head. Second line: Turning palms outward, players wiggle fingers in downward motion. Third line: Raising both hands above their head, they touch fingers, making a sun. Last line: Repeat motions in the first line.

SONG

John Brown Had a Little Indian

ACTIONS

Little kids always get a kick out of this song, and it's helpful when teaching them how to count. Each time a number is sung, children display the right number of fingers.

SONG

One little, two little, three little Indians,
Four little, five little, six little Indians,
Seven little, eight little, nine little Indians,
Ten little Indian boys.
Ten little, nine little, eight little Indians,
Seven little, six little, five little Indians,
Four little, three little, two little Indians,
One little Indian boy.

Little Bo Peep

Lit- tle Bo Peep has lost her sheep And
can't tell where to find them;
Leave them a- lone And they'll come home,
Wag- ging their tails be- hind them.

2. Little Bo Peep fell fast asleep
   And dreamt she heard them
     bleating;
   But when she awoke
   She found it a joke,
   For they were still a fleeting.

3. Then up she took her little crook,
   Determined for to find them;
   She found them indeed,
   But it made her heart bleed,
   For they'd left their tails behind
     them.

4. It happened one day, as Bo Peep
     did stray
   Unto a meadow hard by;
   There she espied
   Their tails, side by side,
   All hung on a tree to dry.

5. She heaved a sigh, and wiped her
     eyes,
   And ran o'er hill and dale,
   And tried what she could
   As a shepherdess should,
   To tack each sheep to its tail.

London Bridge Is Falling Down

This game is most fun when a large group of children participate. Two children acting as *bridge makers* stand an arm's length apart, facing each other. They agree beforehand which items they will choose — sticks or stones, iron or steel, bricks or clay and silver or gold. *Bridge makers* begin with arched hands touching.

ACTIONS

Chorus: Bridge makers drop their hands as the players parade through. Verse 1: *Bridge makers* arch one arm and touch hands. *Bridge makers* touch both hands, forming bridge. Verse 2: Players keep marching through the bridge, singing the tune. Verse 3: *Bridge makers* lock a player and rock the child back and forth inside the bridge. The captured player whispers "sticks" or "stones" to *bridge makers* and is told to line up behind the *bridge maker* who chose this item at the beginning. Players resume play, repeating the chorus and actions continuing with the next verse.

SONG

CHORUS

Lon-don Bridge is fal- ling down,   fal- ling down,   fal- ling down.

Lon-don Bridge is   fal- ling down,   My   fair   la-   dy.

Verse same melody as Chorus

1. Build it up with sticks and stones,
   Sticks and stones, sticks and stones.
   Build it up with sticks and stones,
   My fair lady.

2. Sticks and stones will wear away,
   Wear away, wear away.
   Sticks and stones will wear away,
   My fair lady.

3. Take the key and lock 'em up,
   Lock 'em up, lock 'em up.
   Take the key and lock 'em up
   My fair lady.

4. Build it up with iron and steel
   Iron and steel, iron and steel.
   Build it up with iron and steel,
   My fair lady.

5. Iron and steel will rust away,
   Rust away, rust away.
   Iron and steel will rust away,
   My fair lady.
   (Repeat verse 3 and chorus.)

6. Build it up with bricks and clay,
   Bricks and clay, bricks and clay.
   Build it up with bricks and clay,
   My fair lady.

7. Bricks and clay will wash away,
   Wash away, wash away.
   Bricks and clay will wash away,
   My fair lady.
   (Repeat verse 3 and chorus.)

8. Build it up with silver and gold,
   Silver and gold, silver and gold.
   Build it up with silver and gold,
   My fair lady.

9. Silver and gold is stole away,
   Stole away, stole away.
   Silver and gold is stole away,
   My fair lady.
   (Repeat verse 3 and chorus.)

Whichever side has captured the most players wins. The last players captured on each side are the new *bridge makers*.

Mary Had a Little Lamb

2. Everywhere that Mary went,
   Mary went, Mary went,
   Everywhere that Mary went,
   The lamb was sure to go.

3. Followed her to school one day,
   School one day, school one day,
   Followed her to school one day,
   Which was against the rules.

4. Made the children laugh and play,
   Laugh and play, laugh and play.
   Made the children laugh and play,
   To see a lamb at school.

My Mother Told Me

A song that dates back for decades, this old favorite is one little girls love to sing.

Oats, Peas, Beans and Barley Grow

ACTIONS

This old-fashioned singing game always pleases kids because it allows them to act out the words they are singing. Children stand in a circle holding hands. One child acts as the *farmer* and stands in the middle of the circle. Children promenade to the right around the *farmer,* singing. In the first verse, the *farmer* sows seed, stands erect, stands at ease, stamps his or her foot, claps, turns around and shades his or her eyes. At the end of the verse, the *farmer* points to another child, who becomes the new *farmer,* and everyone sings the chorus followed by verse two, etc. This continues in the same way until each child has acted as the *farmer.*

SONG

Verse same melody as Chorus

1. First the farmer sows his seed,
   Stands erect and takes his ease,
   He stamps his foot and claps his hands,
   And turns around to view his lands.
   (Repeat chorus)

2. Next the farmer waters the seed,
   Stands erect and takes his ease,
   He stamps his foot and claps his hands,
   And turns around to view his lands.
   (Repeat chorus)

3. Next the farmer hoes the weeds,
   Stands erect and takes his ease,
   He stamps his foot and claps his hands,
   And turns around to view his lands.
   (Repeat chorus)

4. Last the farmer harvests his seed,
   Stands erect and takes his ease.
   He stamps his foot and claps his hands,
   And turns around to view his lands.
   (Repeat chorus)

Oh, Dear, What Can the Matter Be?

This lovely little song was popular in England at the end of the 18th century. Little girls still love it today.

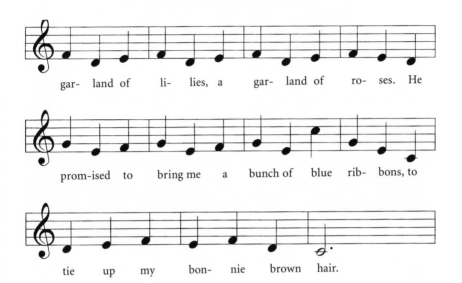

gar- land of   li- lies, a   gar- land of   ro- ses. He

prom-ised to   bring me   a   bunch of   blue   rib- bons, to

tie   up   my   bon- nie   brown   hair.

Oh My Darling Clementine

This is an old ballad that became popular shortly after the Civil War. Kids still love it today as they did then.

1. In a cavern, in a canyon, excavating for a mine,
   Dwelt a miner, forty-niner and his daughter, Clementine.

2. Lite she was and like a fairy and her shoes were number nine;
   Her ring boxes without topses, sandals were for Clementine.
   (Repeat chorus)

3. Drove her ducklings to the water, every morning just at nine;
   Hit her foot against a splinter, fell into the foaming brine.
   (Repeat chorus)

4. Ruby lips above the water, blowing bubbles soft and fine;
   But alas, I was no swimmer, so I lost my Clementine.
   (Repeat chorus)

5. Then the miner, forty-niner soon began to peak and pine;
   Thought he oughter join his daughter now he's with his Clementine.
   (Repeat chorus)

6. In my dreams she still doth haunt me robed in garments soaked in brine.
   Though in life I used to hug her, now she's dead I draw the line.
   (Repeat chorus)

Verse has same melody as Chorus

Old MacDonald Had a Farm

This is one of the best-loved and oldest children's songs. Little kids choose this one any chance they get. Any animals of a child's choice can be mimicked in this song.

2. And on his farm he had a pig,
   (Repeat E-I as above.)
   With an oink, oink here,
   And an oink, oink there, (etc.)

3. And on his farm he had a duck,
   (Repeat E-I as above.)
   With a quack, quack here,
   And a quack, quack there, (etc.)

4. And on his farm he had a sheep,
   (Repeat E-I as above.)
   With a baa, baa here,
   And a baa, baa there, (etc.)

5. And on his farm he had a horse,
   (Repeat E-I as above.)
   With a neigh, neigh here,
   And a neigh, neigh there, (etc.)

6. And on his farm he had a goat,
   (Repeat E-I as above.)
   With a bleat, bleat here,
   And a bleat, bleat there, (etc.)

7. And on his farm he had some chickens,
   (Repeat E-I as above.)
   With a cluck, cluck here,
   And a cluck, cluck there, (etc.)

Playmate

Little girls love to sing this old-time favorite, and it's great to use as a clapping rhythm.

2. Hey, hey, hey playmate,
   I cannot play with you.
   My dolly has the flu,
   Boo hoo, hoo, hoo, hoo, hoo.
   Can't holler down your rain barrel,
   Slide down your cellar door,
   But we'll be jolly friends,
   Forever more.

Pop Goes the Weasel

ACTIONS

Players chosen by the one playing *weasel* act out the role depending on the words of the verse. Players skip to the left during the first verse and chorus as the *weasel* stands in the middle. At the beginning of verse two, the *weasel* tags one child, who acts as the *monkey*. Circle players stand still as the *monkey* then skips around the outside of the circle. The *weasel* follows through the hole and skips after the *monkey*. On the word "Pop," the *weasel* smacks the *monkey* on the bottom, and the *monkey* runs back to his or her place.

The *weasel* chooses a *possum* in the beginning of verse three. The *possum* pretends to pull up the covers. On the word "Pop," the *monkey* tickles the *possum* and the *possum* runs back to opening.

The *weasel* picks a *groundhog* in verse four. The *groundhog* crawls around looking for a hole. On the word "Pop," the *weasel* dashes at the *groundhog*, making a scary face. The *groundhog* runs back to the opening. Players skip to the left at the beginning of each verse until the *weasel* tags someone; then they stand still. No action is called for on the word "Pop" in the chorus.

SONG

(Verse 1 on facing page)

2. All around the cobbler's bench,
   The monkey chased the weasel,
   The monkey thought 'twas all in fun,
   Pop goes the weasel!
   (chorus)

3. The possum pulled the covers up,
   Because he had the measles,
   The quilt began to wiggle and bump,
   Pop goes the weasel!
   (chorus)

4. "It's time for bed," the groundhog says,
   "I'll take it nice and easy."
   But when he crawls into his hole,
   Pop goes the weasel!
   (chorus)

Verse 1

Ring Around the Rosie

ACTIONS

Joining hands, players slowly walk around in a circle while singing the song. On "We all fall down," the last one to sit down is out. The remaining boy or girl after all the others have been eliminated is the winner.

SONG

Row, Row, Row Your Boat

Loads of fun to sing around a campfire or on a bus trip. Two or more persons or groups may join in the singing.

This song is sung as a round and is repeated from the beginning at the end of the stanza. When the first group gets to "Merrily," the second group begins singing "Row..."

Row,   row,   row   your boat,

Gent-   ly   down   the   stream,

Mer- ri-   ly,   mer- ri-   ly,   mer- ri-   ly,   mer- ri-   ly,

Life   is   but   a   dream.

She'll Be Coming Round the Mountain

ACTIONS

The spoken words are acted out as follows: "Toot, toot"—two pulls of a locomotive whistle cord; "Whoa, back"—a long hard pull on the reins; "Hi, babe"—a wave of the hand; "Cockadoodle-doo"—flapping of wings; "Yum, yum"—rubbing the stomach; and "Snore, snore"—snoring sounds.

SONG

She'll be com-ing round the moun-tain when she comes. Toot-Toot She'll be com-ing round the moun-tain when she comes. She'll be com-ing round the moun-tain; She'll be com-ing round the moun-tain; She'll be com-ing round the moun-tain when she comes. Toot-toot (spoken).

2. She'll be driving six white horses
   when she comes. Whoa back.
   (Repeat as before)
   Whoa back, toot-toot.

3. Oh, we'll all go out to meet her
   when she comes. Hi babe!
   (Repeat as before.)
   Hi babe, whoa back, toot-toot.

4. Oh, we'll kill the old red rooster
   when she comes. Cockadoodle-doo.
   (Repeat as before.)
   Cockadoodle-doo, hi babe,
      whoa back, toot-toot.

5. And we'll all have chicken and dumplins
   when she comes. Yum-yum.
   (Repeat as before.)
   Yum-yum, cockadoodle-doo,
      hi babe, whoa back, toot-toot.

6. Oh, she'll have to sleep with grandma
   when she comes. Snore, snore.
   (Repeat as before.)
   Snore, snore, yum-yum,
      cockadoodle-doo, hi babe, whoa back,
      toot-toot.

7. And she'll wear red flannel long johns
   when she comes. Wheee-whooo.
   (Repeat as before.)
   Wheee-whooo, snore, snore,
   cockadoodle-doo, hi babe, whoa back, toot-toot.

Sing a Song of Sixpence

Sing a song of six- pence a   pock-et full of rye;

Four and twen-ty black- birds,   baked   in   a   pie;

When the pie was o-   pened, the birds be- gan to sing;

Was-n't that a dain- ty dish to   set be- fore the king?

2. The king was in the counting house, counting
   out his money;
   The queen was in the parlor, eating bread and honey;
   The maid was in the garden, hanging out the clothes;
   When down came a blackbird and snipped off her nose.

Skip to My Lou

ACTIONS

Children stand in a circle, with one child in the middle. When the singing starts, the middle child chooses a partner, and they skip around inside the circle as the others sing and clap. Chorus: On the fourth line, the middle child joins the circle, and the first child chosen remains in the middle. Verses: The player in the middle skips around the inside of the circle while others sing the verse. On the fourth line, the middle player picks a partner, and the chorus is repeated as they both skip around inside the circle. At the last line of the chorus, the middle player returns to the circle, and the partner remains in the middle.

SONG

Verse same melody as Chorus

1. Lost my partner, what'll I do?
   Lost my partner, what'll I do?
   Lost my partner, what'll I do?
   Skip to my Lou, my darling.
   (Repeat chorus)

2. I'll get another one prettier than you;
   I'll get another one prettier than you;
   I'll get another one prettier than you;
   Skip to my Lou, my darling.
   (Repeat chorus)

3. Flies in the buttermilk, shoo, fly shoo;
   Flies in the buttermilk, shoo, fly shoo;
   Flies in the buttermilk, shoo, fly shoo;
   Skip to my Lou, my darling.
   (Repeat chorus)

4. Cows in the barnyard, moo, moo, moo;
   Cows in the barnyard, moo, moo, moo;
   Cows in the barnyard, moo, moo, moo;
   Skip to my Lou, my darling.
   (Repeat chorus)

5. Train is a coming, choo, choo, choo;
   Train is a coming, choo, choo, choo;
   Train is a coming, choo, choo, choo;
   Skip to my Lou, my darling.

There's a Hole in My Bucket

This is a great song for boys and girls to sing parts. Boys sing the part of *Willie*; girls sing *Liza's* lines.

WILLIE: There's a hole in my buck- et, dear Li- za, dear Li- za. There's a hole in my buck- et, dear Li- za, a hole.

LIZA: Mend the hole, then, dear Willie, dear Willie, you silly.
       Mend the hole, then, dear Willie, you silly, mend it.

WILLIE: With what shall I mend it, dear Liza, dear Liza?
        With what shall I mend it, dear Liza, with what?

LIZA: With a straw, then, dear Willie, dear Willie, you silly,
       With a straw, then, dear Willie, dear Willie, with a straw.

WILLIE: But the straw is too long, dear Liza, dear Liza.
        But the straw is too long, dear Liza, then what?

LIZA: Cut the straw, then, dear Willie, dear Willie, you silly.
       Cut the straw, then, dear Willie, you silly cut the straw.

WILLIE: With what shall I cut it, dear Liza, dear Liza?
        With what shall I cut it, dear Liza, with what?

LIZA: With a knife, then, dear Willie, dear Willie, you silly.
       With a knife, then, dear Willie, you silly, with a knife.

WILLIE: But the knife is too dull, dear Liza, dear Liza.
        But the knife is too dull, dear Liza, then what?

LIZA: Whet the knife, then, dear Willie, dear Willie, you silly.
Whet the knife, then, dear Willie, you silly, whet it.

WILLIE: With what will I whet it, dear Liza, dear Liza?
With what will I whet it, dear Liza, with what?

LIZA: With a stone, then, dear Willie, dear Willie, you silly.
With a stone, then, dear Willie, dear Willie, with a stone.

WILLIE: But the stone is too rough, dear Liza, dear Liza.
But the stone is too rough, dear Liza, then what?

LIZA: Smooth the stone, then, dear Willie, dear Willie, you silly.
Smooth the stone, then, dear Willie, you silly, smooth it.

WILLIE: With what shall I smooth it, dear Liza, dear Liza?
With what shall I smooth it, dear Liza, with what?

LIZA: With water, then, dear Willie, dear Willie, you silly.
With water, then, dear Willie, you silly, with water.

WILLIE: In what shall I carry it, dear Liza, dear Liza?
In what shall I carry it, dear Liza, in what?

LIZA: In a bucket, then, dear Willie, dear Willie, you silly.
In a bucket, then, dear Willie, you silly, in a bucket.

WILLIE: But there's a hole in my bucket, dear Liza, dear Liza.
But there's a hole in my bucket, dear Liza, a hole.

LIZA: (Spoken) Then mend it, oh Willie!

This Old Man

This delightfully funny song has charmed children for many, many years. Children sit in a circle and pretend to tap on whatever item is being sung about from each verse.

2. This old man, he played two;
   He played knick knack on my *shoe,*
   (Repeat lines three, four and five here
   and at the end of each verse.)

3. This old man, he played three;
   He played knick knack on my *knee,*
   (etc.)

4. This old man, he played four;
   He played knick knack on my *door,*
   (etc.)

5. This old man, he played five;
   He played knick knack on my *hive,*
   (etc.)

6. This old man, he played six;

   He played knick knack on my *sticks,*
   (etc.)

7. This old man, he played seven;
   He played knick knack up in *heaven,*
   (etc.)

8. This old man, he played eight;
   He played knick knack on my *gate,*
   (etc.)

9. This old man, he played nine;
   He played knick knack on my *line,*
   (etc.)

10. This old man, he played ten;
    He played knick knack all over
    again, (etc.)

Three Blind Mice

Over 350 years old, this is a classic that may be sung as a round. The *first group* begins and sings the song to the end and repeats from the beginning.

When the *first group* begins to sing, "They all run...," *group two* begins singing from the beginning of the song to the end and repeats.

Three   blind   mice,

Three   blind   mice,

See   how   they   run;

See   how   they   run ———————.   They

all   run af- ter   the   farm- er's   wife;   She

cut off their tails with a carv- ing knife; Did

you ev- er see such a sight in your life, As

three blind mice.

A Tisket, a Tasket
(Drop the Handkerchief)

ACTIONS

Little boys and girls always find this old-fashioned singing game exciting. Players sit in a circle while one player, *it*, skips around the outside of the ring holding a handkerchief while singing the song. When *it* says, "It was you," he or she drops the handkerchief behind another player's back. That child must rise and race around the circle in the opposite direction trying to get back to his or her place before *it* does. If the player succeeds, *it* remains *it*. If *it* fills the opening first, the other player becomes the new *it*.

SONG

A tis-ket, a tas-ket, A green and yel-low bas-ket, I sent a let-ter to my love, And on the way I dropped it. I dropped it, I dropped it, I dropped it from my bas-ket. A lit-tle child has picked it up and put it in your pock-et.

(Spoken: It wasn't you, it wasn't you,... etc. It was you!)

Two, Four, Nine

Kids always get a big kick out of this old-fashioned song. No wonder it's been around for generations.

It also encourages them not to smoke.

Two, four, nine, the goose drank wine. The

mon- key smoked to- bac- co in the street car line. The

line broke; they all be- gan to choke. They

all went to heav- en but the lit- tle bil- ly goat.

Where Is Thumbkin?

ACTIONS

This is a super song that teaches little kids coordination and the names of their fingers. Two rows of children, with their hands behind their backs, stand facing each other. Each player on *team one* pulls his or her right hand out, holding up the thumb and sings, "Where is thumbkin?" Each player on *team two* pulls out his or her right hand, holding up the thumb, and answers, "Here I am." Thumbs bow to each other, and on "Run and hide," all players hide their hands behind their backs. The players continue, using the pointer finger up through the pinkie. *Team one* sings the questions, and *team two* sings the answers.

SONG

2. Where is pointer? Where is pointer?
   (Repeat as in verse 1.)

3. Where is middle? Where is middle?
   (Repeat as before.)

4. Where is ringer? Where is ringer?
   (Repeat as before.)

5. Where is pinkie? Where is pinkie?
   (Repeat as before.)

Yankee Doodle

Yan-kee— Doo- dle   went to   town a-   ri-   din' on   a   po-   ny;   He stuck   a   feath- er   in   his   cap   and   called it   mac- a-   ro-   ni.

CHORUS

Yan-   kee Doo- dle   keep   it   up,   Yan-   kee Doo- dle   dan-   dy;   Mind   the mu- sic   and   the   step, and   with   the   girls   be   han-   dy.

2. Father and I went down to camp
   Along with Captain Gooding,
   And there we saw the men and
     boys,
   As thick as hasty pudding.
   (Chorus)

3. The troopers, they would gallop up
   And fire right in our faces;

It scared me almost half to death
To see them run such races.
(Chorus)

4. I can't tell you but half I saw,
   They kept up such a smother;
   I took my hat off, made a bow,
   And scampered home to Mother.
   (Chorus)

You Are My Sunshine

You are my sun- shine, My on- ly

sun- shine; You make me hap- py

When skies are gray. You'll nev- er

know dear, How much I love you;

Please don't take my sun- shine a

way.

2. The other night dear,
   As I lay sleeping,
   I dreamt I held you in my arms.
   When I awoke, dear, I was mistaken,
   And I hung my head and cried.
   (Repeat verse one.)

Party
Games

Air, Water, Fire

A pastime that is a hit with older kids, this one keeps youngsters enthralled for quite a long time. Players sit in a circle, with one player who is *it* in the center. *It* points to a player and calls out "Air," "Water" or "Fire" and quickly counts to ten. The player pointed to must say the name of a creature living in the element named before the count of ten, except for "Fire," when the player should remain quiet. For example, if *it* cries "Air," the player might respond "eagle" or some other animal of the air. The player might respond "goldfish" if *it* calls "Water."

Once a response is given, it can't be used again by another player. *It* continues until a player pointed to fails to answer correctly before *it* has counted to ten or the player mentions an animal already named. When a player answers incorrectly or responds after *it* has counted to ten, this player is the next *it*.

Balloon Ball

Boys and girls have a great time playing this game which involves two teams. It's played on a rectangular table with the narrow ends of the table acting as goal lines. A balloon is placed in the center of the table. The teams try to blow the balloon up to or through their opponent's goal. Teams score one point when the balloon touches the goal line and six points if the balloon is blown through the goal and off the table. No one may touch the balloon at any time. If the balloon happens to be blown off the sides of the table, it is replaced in the center across from the place where it went off. The first team to score ten points wins.

Blind Bell

This is a super party game that kids have been fond of for many, many years. Every player except one is blindfolded. The player without the blindfold wears a ribbon around his or her neck with a bell tied to it. As this player moves, the bell sounds and all the blindfolded players try to tag him or her. It's a lot harder than one would think to dodge the blindfolded players. The first player to tag the one wearing the bell wears it in the next round.

Blind Man's Buff

This game dates back hundreds of years, and kids find it as exciting today as their ancestors once did. A player is chosen, blindfolded, turned around three times in the center of the room and left there. Other players dance around *blind man*, calling and dodging out of *blind man's* way to avoid being captured. When *blind man* catches a player, he or she has three guesses to name the person. If *blind man* guesses right, the player caught is the new *blind man*. If wrong, he or she continues to be *blind man* and tries to catch another player.

Blowing Feathers

Both younger and older kids have fun galore playing this enchanting game. Two or more teams line up, and each team is given a feather. When a signal is given, the feathers are tossed in the air. Players blow at their team's feather, trying to keep it from falling to the ground. The team whose feather drops to the ground first loses.

Bobbing for Apples

This humorous, popular game is a favorite at Halloween parties. A large tub half-filled with water is set on the floor. Lots of apples are thrown in the tub and float in the water. Everyone has a turn trying to pick up an apple with his teeth. Kneeling down, the player bends over the tub with hands clasped behind his back, attempting to pick up the apple in his teeth and lift it out of the tub with hands still clasped. This feat is much easier when the player can push the apple with his chin until the apple rests against one side of the tub. This makes it simpler for the player to grab the apple. Players are timed; the player who nabs the most apples is the winner.

Button, Button

This old-time game is always a favorite with kids at a party. Sitting in a circle, players place their hands out in front of them, palms pressed together. Inside the circle, one child stands with his or her hands in the same position except that he or she is holding a button. This player walks around the circle, pushing his or her hands between each of the other player's hands. Eventually, the button is passed to another pair of hands. After circling the group, he or she points to a player (not the one who now has the button) and says, "Button, button, who's got the button?"

The child pointed to must guess who has the button. If correct, he or she then takes the button around the circle and play resumes. If incorrect, the one guessed must open his or her hands, showing that they are empty. Then the player guessed has a chance to guess who has the button, and the game continues until the button is found and another round is played.

Buzz

This exciting counting game should be played at a fast pace by older children who have adding skills. Players sit in a circle. One player begins by counting "one"; the next says, "two" and so on around the group. When the word "seven" is reached, the word "buzz" is substituted. Multiples of seven should also be skipped and the word "buzz" used. For example, for fourteen, "teen buzz" would be substituted. The following player says "fifteen." Counting continues with "buzz" being said for "seven" anytime it is contained in a number, such as "buzzteen" for "seventeen," or "twenty-buzz" for 27.

Cahoots

This is a party game older boys and girls go for in a big way. Two players are in "Cahoots": One, the *leader*, stays with the rest of the group, and the other, his or her *partner,* volunteers to go out of the room. After the group chooses an object in the room, the *partner* is brought back. Then the *leader* asks, "Is it this vase?" "Is it this picture?" The *partner* always shakes his or her head no. When the *leader* points to the chosen object and says, "Is it that book?" the *partner* nods "yes," to the amazement of the other players. The clue is given when the *leader* says "that" instead of "this."

Players try to determine how the partner knew which object to pick. Players do not reveal their guesses. When a player thinks he or she knows the trick, that player becomes the new *partner.* Frequently, the player's idea is all wrong. If this happens, the original *partner* then goes out again. If the player is right, however, this player may take the *partner's* place until someone else guesses the trick.

Cat and Mice

This is a fun tag game that allows little kids to pretend while playing the game. Every player but one, who is *cat*, chooses a seat around the room. *Cat* hunches under a table in the middle of the room saying, "Meow." Five children are chosen as the *mice*; other players must wait until their turn. Once *cat* is under the table, *mice* approach, scratching and making scraping mice sounds. *Cat* springs forward, crying "meow," trying to tag one of the *mice* before he or she returns to his or her seat.

The game is more exciting if the *mice* scurry around the room before running back to their seats. If one of the *mice* is tagged, he or she has to be the next *cat*, and the first *cat* then joins the *mice*. If *cat* doesn't tag another player, he or she is *cat* in the next round. In the next round, new *mice* are chosen, giving every child a chance to play.

Clothespins in the Jar

A good choice for any children's party, this game is simple and never fails to delight kids. All that is needed is a small mouthed jar and ten clothespins. One by one, each player attempts to drop the clothespins from his or her nose level into the jar. The player who drops the most clothespins into the jar is the winner.

Coffeepot

This guessing game is a big hit with school-aged kids. One player is chosen to be the *guesser* and leaves the room while the other players select an action word, such as, eat, dance, jump, swim, sleep, bake, whistle, etc. When the player returns to the room, he or she tries to guess the word. *Guesser* may ask any player any question he or she wishes as long as the word "coffeepot" is used instead of the word the *guesser* is trying to guess. Players must respond truthfully, although they must also substitute the word "coffeepot" instead of the action word chosen.

If the chosen word is "dive," the guesser may ask each player a question in turn, for example, "Do you coffeepot at school?" The player would respond, "No, I can't coffeepot at school?" or "Teacher won't let me coffeepot at school." Other example questions might be: "Do you coffeepot outside?" "Do you coffeepot in bed?" "Do you coffeepot in the park?" "Do you coffeepot at the table." In the long run, the *guesser* will eventually guess the correct word, in most cases. When this happens, the player whose answer gave the word away is now the new *guesser*, or if a *guesser* fails to guess the correct word after five minutes, another player may take a turn as the *guesser*.

Ditto

This silly game instigates the giggles in kids. Players all sit in a circle; one player acts as *leader*. Other players must do what *leader* does but may not talk or laugh. *Leader* makes all the actions while seated. *Leader* might stick out his or her tongue, take off his or her shoe and wiggle a toe, pull the nose, ear or chin of another player, tickle another player, etc. *Leader* may laugh, but other players must not. *Leader* does everything possible to make others laugh. When a player laughs, he or she is out of the game. The last player to remain is the next *leader*.

Do as I Say

Player who is *it* sits before a line of players, giving them orders. *It* points to his or her chin, saying "chin, chin, chin," and other players must do the same. Then *it* might point to his or her nose and say, "nose, nose, nose," and the rest must do likewise. This continues, with *it* pointing to other parts of the face and head, until suddenly *it* announces one part of the face and head but points to another. For example, *it* says "eyes" while pointing to his or her cheeks. Other players must touch their eyes, not their cheeks.

Any player who doesn't follow the command sits out, until there is only one surviving player. This player is the next *it*. The game is a lot of fun when *it* gives orders quickly.

Drawing in the Dark

Each player is given a pencil and paper. The lights are turned out, and everyone is asked to draw the same picture, such as a house. After everyone has drawn the house, they are asked to add a tree, then a fence around the house, flowers in the garden, etc. The lights are turned on again, and the strange masterpieces are shown. Lots of laughter can be expected when children view each other's works of art.

Duck, Duck, Goose

Especially fun with preschoolers up through eight-year-olds, this game of chase works indoors as well as outdoors. Children stand in a circle. One child, *it*, runs around the outside of the circle randomly tagging players on top of the head chanting, "Duck, Duck, Duck, Duck, Duck, Duck." Whenever *it* shouts "Goose" and tags a player on the head, the tagged player must circle around the opposite direction of the outside player and return to the open spot before *it* does. If *it* has filled the spot, the tagged player becomes the next *it*. If the tagged player fills the spot first, *it* remains and play begins once more.

Ducks Fly

This is an interesting and fun follow-the-leader game that kids like a lot. The player who is the *leader* faces the other players, who stand in a half circle around the *leader*. Then the *leader* says "ducks fly" and waves his or her arms, and other players must quickly wave their arms. The *leader* then gives another direction, for example, "horses gallop," "lions roar," "deer run," "rabbits hop," "fish swim," etc. After each command, the *leader* performs the action that he or she named, and all the players imitate the actions.

Any player who does not follow the direction is out as is anyone the *leader* can trick into performing a false action. For example, the *leader* may say "pigs cackle" and cackle like a hen. The players must not follow the action and must remain still until the *leader* gives them a correct command. Lots of snickering and laughs occur in this game.

Eggshell Race

This good party game is a hit with youngsters of every age. Kids should be ready for lots of laughs. Each player is given an empty eggshell. Eggshells can be prepared beforehand by piercing small holes in both ends of the eggs, allowing the white and yolk to drip out. The shells are placed at one end of the room, and a goal is set at the other end. Along with the eggshell, each player is also given a straw. Players must blow the eggshell to the goal without touching the shell. Eggshells blown in this manner move haphazardly, and the game is nearly as much fun to watch as it is to play. The player whose eggshell reaches the goal first wins.

Farmer Is Coming

This exciting game has kids scrambling for a seat. The game begins with each child choosing a seat in the room. A player acting as the *farmer* is in the next room. After counting slowly to 20, all the players tiptoe into the next room and get as close to *farmer* as they dare, trying to surround him or her. The *farmer* claps suddenly, and the others must stand motionless. As soon as the *leader* cries, "The *farmer* is coming," players must dash for their seats in the other room before the *farmer* tags them. Whomever the *farmer* tags is *farmer* in the next game. If the *farmer* fails to tag someone, he or she is *farmer* again.

Feelings

This fun game is played in a dark room. A basement party room works great. The player who is *it* goes to a corner of the room and counts to 100 by fives while other players hide. *It* must catch somebody in the dark and try to guess who the person is. Players try to disguise themselves by putting on other player's glasses, speaking in an uncommon voice or doing other things to deceive *it*. If *it* correctly guesses the caught player, that player becomes *it*. If incorrect, the original *it* remains to take another turn.

Finger in the Bucket

A game that is sure to cause hysterics at any party, this silly pastime is loads of fun when ten or more players participate. All players sit on the floor at random around the room, allowing at least an arm's length between players. One player is the *caller* and directs the actions that the other players must follow. The *caller* and all players form their left hands into a loose fist, forming a circle with the fingers and thumb, resembling a bucket with a hole in it or resembling an hour glass if held up to one's eyes.

The *caller* begins the game by stating what action the players should perform; the caller acts it out, and the players must follow the *caller's* instruction and imitate that action. For example, the *caller* cries, "Finger in the bucket" and sticks his or her finger in his or her bucket and all players must follow this example. Then the *caller* might state, "Out of the bucket" and the players must pull their fingers from their finger holes.

The *caller* continues directing the other players: "Finger in the bucket"; Finger out of the bucket"; "Out of the bucket"; "In the bucket"; "In the bucket"; "Out of the bucket." When the *caller* states, "In somebody else's bucket," the *caller* pulls his or her bucket away, leaving one player short, as in Musical Chairs. All the players scramble across the floor trying to find another bucket to put their fingers in. Players must crawl and must not stand up to get to another player. The player who can't find a "bucket" to put his or her finger in is out. This includes the *caller*.

The *caller* continues to call and direct until he or she is out. Then, any other player who is still in the game may volunteer to be the new *caller*, and the game continues until there are only two remaining players, who are the winners.

Fire in the Mountain

This crowd-pleaser, similar to Musical Chairs or Duck, Duck, Goose, always earns children's laughter and enthusiasm. Players form two circles, one inside and the other outside with players in the outside circle standing directly behind a player on the inside circle. This game is most fun when there are at least five or more children in each circle. Another player, *it*, stands in the center of the inside circle and calls out;

> Fire in the mountain,
> Fire like the sun,
> Fire in the mountain,
> Run, run, run!

While *it* is chanting, players in the outer ring must run in a circle around the inside group without joining hands. While *it* calls out, she, along with the players inside the circle, slowly clap their hands. *It* repeats the rhyme until, suddenly, *it* stops and holds up her hands high in the air. Inside players do the same. *It* then races to get a place in the outside circle, behind a player in the inner circle. Circling players in the outside group do the same thing. The player who doesn't find a place is *it* in the next round.

Fish Race

This is a breathlessly exciting relay game. Players divide into teams, with each player having a plastic straw and each team a paper fish. The first player on each team holds the fish at the end of the straw by sucking in or inhaling and passes the fish to the next teammate by blowing out as the other teammate inhales. The fish is passed from one player to another in this way until one team wins by finishing first.

Fisherman

A fun game for older children, this one is good on a rainy day when kids are bored. The thrill is in catching another by snagging the player in a string. Players sit at a table. One player acts as the *fisherman*, holding a stick approximately ten inches long with a string tied to it. The end of the string is tied in a loop about eight inches around. The *fisherman* holds the stick so that the loop of string lies flat in the center of the table.

When the *fisherman* cries "fish," all the children must put the pointer finger of their right hand into the loop. Without warning the *fisherman* calls "fish" again, quickly pulling up the stick. As fast as possible, players pull their fingers away. Any player whose finger gets caught in the string is charged with a point. After all players take a turn as *fisherman*, the player with the least number of points wins.

Frog in the Sea

This is one of the few tag games that work well indoors. Younger kids have a croaking good time with this one. All players stand in a circle, with the child designated as *frog* sitting in the middle of the circle with his or her legs crossed. Circle players chant:

> Frog in the middle,
> Frog in the sea,
> Frog in the puddle,
> Can't catch me.

The children run as close to *frog* as they dare. *Frog* tries to tag them while remaining in a seated, crossed-legged position. *Frog* may bend and stretch over, reaching as far as possible while attempting to tag a player. This goes on until *frog* tags another player. The tagged player then must be *frog* in the next game.

Fruit Basket

Kids like this fun party game, which is similar to Puss in the Corner. There should be one less corner (or other bases) than number of players. One child is chosen *it* and stands in the middle of the room. All other players take a corner/base. Each one chooses a different fruit and identifies it to the others. *It* then calls out the name of two of the fruits that players have named. The players who have named those fruits then must exchange corners/bases quickly before *it* grabs one of their vacated spots. If *it* succeeds, the one left without a corner/base is the new *it*, and the old *it* takes the fruit of the player who was just there.

Play continues, with a different pair of fruits being called each time. To shake things up and generate added excitement, *it* can occasionally call out "Fruit Basket!" Then, everyone must find a different corner/base while *it* attempts to occupy one, leaving someone without a corner/base. This game ends when players tire of it, or a group could play until each child has taken a turn as *it*.

Geography

For this challenging game, children have great fun using their thinking skills. The first player names any place that has an actual geographical location — a city, state, country, river, lake, ocean, mountain, etc. The next child continues by using the last letter of the place named as the first letter of the place he or she will name. For example, the first player might name "Egypt." The next player might say "Texas." Since a place can be named only once, sometimes a player can't think of a new location and is out. Often, the game ends with only two or three survivors.

Gossip

People are often guilty of misinterpreting what they hear. This long-loved favorite game proves the fact. The game works best with a large group of kids — ages six and older. This game develops creativity in youngsters and in the end generates loads of laughter.

Players sit in a circle; the first player makes up a sentence and whispers the "gossip" into the next person's ear. For example, "The spider crept across the teacup to see the roach back-swimming in the soup tureen." This player quickly whispers the line to the next one, and this continues around the circle.

The last child must reveal what he or she was told. The phrase may end up with the last player stating, "A tiger leapt over a stump, watching the coach sink in the lagoon." Kids always laugh at the ending response. Each player takes a turn at starting the "gossip."

Grandmother's Trunk

Although this game is challenging, kids that possess good spelling and memory skills always have a grand time playing it. Everyone sits in a circle. The first player starts by saying, "I packed my grandmother's trunk and in it I put an _____." The player puts in an item beginning with the letter *A*, for example, "I packed my grandmother's trunk and in it I put an apricot." The next player repeats this phrase and adds something beginning with *B*.

The game progresses alphabetically, with each player repeating the phrase — including everything already put in the trunk — and adding another item. If a player can't think of all the things in the right order, that player is out. The following player begins with the next letter of the alphabet, and play starts once more. The game ends at *Z*.

Guess the Beans

This guessing game has been played at parties for more years than is known and kids love it. One of the hardest parts of this game is done not by the players but by the person who has to count the beans that are put into the jar before the game begins. A quart or gallon jar or large glass vase may be used to hold whatever item is desired: dried soup beans, black-eyed peas, jelly beans, pennies, cotton balls, etc. Each player tries to guess how many items are inside the jar. The player who guesses correctly or the closest to the right number wins. Normally, a prize is given to the winner.

Guess Who?

There are various methods of playing this delightful game. The player chosen as *it* must guess the name of another player. *It* stands with his or her back to the group or wears a blindfold; a player quietly steps forward and pokes a finger into *its* back, asking, "Guess Who?" Children may disguise their voices in order to fool *it*. Then *it* has three chances to guess the player's identity. If *it* guesses correctly, the other player becomes *it*. If wrong, *it* remains *it*, and another child tries to get *it* to guess who he or she is.

Sometimes a sheet is strung across the room; *it* stands on one side of the sheet, and the players are on the other side. In the sheet a hole is cut big enough for a player to stick his or her nose through. *It* must guess which player's nose this is. Players may also put one of their eyes to the hole, and *it* tries to guess which child it is. Older kids as well as younger children enjoy this one.

Ha! Ha!

Kids get the hysterics in this game, but they can't laugh or they are out. Players stand in a circle. One person starts by saying something ridiculous to the player to the left and adding "ha" to the end of it. The sillier the saying, the better. For example, "Greasy, grimy gopher guts. Ha!" The next person repeats the saying to the player to the left and adds "ha, ha." The third player does likewise, adds "ha, ha, ha," and so on. Players may not laugh or smile. Whenever a player laughs, that player is eliminated. The game continues until there is only one survivor — the winner.

Here's the Church

Little children love to watch this game; however, most children don't possess the coordination skills to perform this action until they are four years of age or older. Placing hands back to back with fingers spread, interlock fingers and bend them while turning palms to face each other. Thumbs remain upright, forming the church door in front of the interlaced fingers, with the knuckles forming the church roof. Raising the index fingers, press them together to form the church steeple. Part the thumbs to open the church door. Bring the backs of the hands together, straighten the fingers and wiggle them, showing the people.

> Here's the church.
> Here's the steeple.
> Open the door.
> Here's the people.

Hidden Treasures

This is a good game to play detective. Players are given a list of 20 items hidden in the house. Objects can be anything — such as a particular book, hair clip, matchbook, lipstick tube, etc. All the items are visible but cleverly concealed. Each player tries to locate the objects, noting where they were found. The first player to locate all the items is the winner.

Hide the Thimble

This enjoyable game keeps kids happily occupied for a long time. One player is shown a small object, such as a thimble, or pen. Then this child is sent out of the room while the others hide the object. When the object is hidden, they call, "Ready!"

The player who is in the other room returns to hunt for the object. The other players give clues, saying, "You're cooler," or "warmer," or "freezing," letting him or her know if the object is close or far away. When the object is near, the clue is "warmer"; if the item is far away, the clue is "cooler," etc. After this player finds the object, another child is sent out of the room, and the game is repeated until everyone has had a chance to look for the hidden item.

Hold Fast, Let Go

Older boys and girls like this fast-paced pastime. One player acts as the *caller*. Every child holds a rubber ball. Standing in a line, players face the *caller*, who says either, "Hold Fast!" or "Let Go!" Players must do the exact opposite of what the *caller* says. Randomly, the *caller* may try to confuse players by dropping his or her ball when announcing "Let Go!" or by holding on to it while saying "Hold Fast!" It's much more exciting when the *caller* calls quickly. Also, it's better for the caller to give the same order several times in a row and then suddenly change. Players who perform the same act that the *caller* says are out. The last player to remain is the new *caller*.

Hot Potato

Years ago, a potato actually was used to play this game. Little boys and girls have a good time playing this game today using a potato, ball or any small item. As in musical chairs, music is played while the players sit in a circle and quickly pass the item from one player to the next. When the music stops, the child holding the "potato" is out. The last player left in the game wins.

How Many Words?

Here's a good word game for youngsters who can read and spell. Each player needs a pencil and a sheet of paper. Players decide on a long word and are given a time limit (five or ten minutes) to write down as many words as possible using only the letters in the long word. Proper nouns don't count. Following is an example:

CHRONOLOGICALLY:

lag	cry	gail	gaily	all	crying	goal	call	lily	cain
log	chilly	chain	clog	rich	can	along	hall	ill	long
no	nag	rig	hog	lag	gall	chain	nigh	gill	rain
con	grill	lain	roll	lying	gray	nail	gag	rail	rig
logic	lay	in	on	chronic	chill	local	hill	ally	chronology
an	ago	logo	go	gay	logical	hay	ray	rally	laying

The player who writes down the most words at the end of the time period wins.

Hunt the Slipper

Boys and girls get a kick out of this funny game. All players are *cobblers* except one, who is the *customer*. *Cobblers* sit on the floor, and the *customer* gives one of her shoes (a cardboard cutout shaped like a shoe may be substituted) to a *cobbler*. The *customer* says: "Cobbler, Cobbler, mend my shoe. Get it done by half past two." The *customer* turns around and counts to ten while the *cobblers* try to conceal the shoe by slyly passing it from one player to another.

When through counting, the *customer* quickly turns, demands the shoe and is told it is not ready. The *customer* tries to find the shoe. The *cobbler* holding the shoe must try to pass it without being caught. When the *customer* does find the shoe, the *cobbler* holding it becomes the next *customer*.

I Am Very Tall

This guessing game works well with children in preschool on up to the early elementary grades. Players stand in a circle while one blindfolded player stands in the middle. One player in the outer circle acts as *leader* and gives a signal: thumbs up if the group is going to be "short" (stooping) or thumbs down if they will be "tall" (standing). *Leader* announces, "Sometimes I am tall; I am very tall. Sometimes I am short; I am very short. Guess what I am now?" When *leader* says "now," the center player tries to guess whether the group is short or tall.

Players in the outer circle should watch carefully making sure to do as the *leader* directs. If center player is wrong, he or she must guess again in the next round. If the blindfolded child is right, he or she selects another player to be blindfolded, and the game continues.

I Love My Love

This game is challenging for girls and boys who know how to spell. Players sit in a circle. One player starts by saying, for example, "I love my love with an *A* because love is annoying." The second player quickly says something else beginning with the letter *A*, such as " I love my love with an *A* because his name is Allen," or " I love my love with an *A* because he is from Argentina." This continues around the circle until every child has named something beginning with *A*.

Then players begin with the letter *B* and the game goes on down through the alphabet. When a player can't think of a word beginning with the right letter, he or she is out. The game should move quickly, with little or no hesitation between players. Players who stay in the game the longest win.

I Say

Little boys and girls have a great time playing this game. A *leader* stands before the other players and says, "I say skip," or "I say jump," or any action. If *leader* does not say "I say" before a command, players must not perform the action. For example, if *leader* says "hop," players shouldn't hop because *leader* didn't say "I say hop." To confuse players, sometimes *leader* does some other action than named, such as jumping when the command was to kneel. Players performing actions different from what *leader* says or acting when "I say" didn't precede the command are out. The last remaining player becomes the new *leader*.

Jack Be Nimble

Little children get a big kick out of this jumping game. Standing in a line, players take turns jumping over a small box or bottle, which represents a candlestick, as they chant:

Jack be nimble,
Jack be quick,
Jack jump over the candlestick.

If a child knocks over the "candlestick," he or she is out of the game. The player who stays in the longest wins. If all are good jumpers, play continues until they choose to end the game.

Jerusalem and Jericho

This is a game little children love to play. The player acting as *leader* stands in front of the others, who are lined up in a single row. When *leader* calls out "Jerusalem!" players must bow very deeply. Whenever *leader* yells "Jericho!" no player may move. *Leader* tries to catch players doing the wrong thing at the wrong time. For example, *leader* might bow when saying "Jericho!" or might prolong the first syllable and end the command quickly — "Jee e e err rusalem!" or "Jee e e err richo!" Players who move at the wrong time or fail to move at the right time are out. Last player to survive is the new *leader*.

Kaleidoscope

This game delights little boys and girls. It also helps develop their memory skills while providing a fun time. It's better to have a large number of kids participate in this game. All players are assigned a number. Each number is written individually on a small piece of paper, and all the pieces of paper are placed in a dish. After six or eight numbers are drawn out, the players assigned those numbers line up in front of the other children.

Then the players standing in front each choose a different color, and one after the other they state what color they have picked. Other players turn away and cover their eyes as the front players change places. The other players turn around and one by one take turns trying to guess the correct colors of the front players, placing them back in the original order.

Players who guess the correct colors and place them in the right order may take a turn as the front player. Even if some players don't succeed in accomplishing this, they should be given a chance to be a front player. Other topics besides colors can be chosen, for example, animals, birds, flowers, insects, trees, etc.

Keep Moving

Boys and girls love this fast-moving game which is played for the hilarity it causes. There is no winner or loser. Normally, an adult leads this game. Players are seated.

The *leader* chants the verses, while holding up whatever body parts are called out and moving them up and down or side to side as the children follow along.

> One finger, one thumb, keep moving,
> One finger, one thumb, keep moving,
> One finger, one thumb, keep moving,
> We'll all be happy again.

The following verses substitute the following lines:

> Two fingers, two thumbs, keep moving.
> Four fingers, two thumbs, keep moving.
> Six fingers, two thumbs, keep moving.
> Eight fingers, two thumbs, keep moving.
> Eight fingers, two thumbs, one hand, keep moving.
> Eight fingers, two thumbs, two hands, keep moving.
> Eight fingers, two thumbs, two hands, one arm,
> keep moving.
> Eight fingers, two thumbs, two hands, two arms,
> keep moving.
> Eight fingers, two thumbs, two hands, two arms,
> one foot, keep moving.
> Eight fingers, two thumbs, two hands, two arms,
> two feet, keep moving.
> Eight fingers, two thumbs, two hands, two arms,
> two feet, one leg, keep moving.
> Eight fingers, two thumbs, two hands, two arms
> two feet, two legs, keep moving.
> Eight fingers, two thumbs, two hands, two arms,
> two feet, two legs, one head, keep moving, we'll
> all be happy again.

In the first line, the *leader* holds up the right pointer finger and right thumb and moves them up and down. For the next verse, the *leader* waves thumbs and forefingers on both hands. In verse three, he or she wiggles both thumbs and two fingers on each hand, etc. Players follow along as quickly as possible.

This silly pastime gives children a good amount of exercise even though they are seated.

Lost Child

One person (normally an adult) acts as *leader*. Children sit randomly around the room. *Leader* chooses one to be *it*. When *it* leaves the room, *leader* chooses one of the children to hide in the room. Then the other players quickly change seats. *It* is called back, and before *leader* slowly counts to five, *it* must guess who is missing. If *it* guesses right, the missing player becomes the next it. If *it* guesses wrong, he or she must be *it* again. Young children really love this game.

Mother Cat

Toddlers through kindergarten-aged boys and girls get a great kick out of playing this inside hide-and-seek game. It also allows them to act out a part. One player is *mother cat*; the other players are *baby kittens*. The game begins when *mother cat* pretends to fall asleep while the *baby kittens* go and hide. When *mother cat* wakes up to find the *baby kittens* missing, she calls, "Meow!" *Baby kittens* answer, "Mew!"

Mother cat must find the *baby kittens* by sound. She continues to call "meow" as they respond "mew" until all of the *baby kittens* are found. The last one found is *mother cat* in the next turn.

Musical Chairs

This is one of the best-loved children's games. Chairs are lined up in a row in the middle of the room. There should be one less chair than the number of players. When the music begins, players circle around the chairs, dancing. As soon as the music stops, each player tries to sit on a seat. The player without a seat is out. One chair is removed and the music starts again. This continues until only one chair and two players remain. On the last round, the player to regain the seat is the winner.

My Name Is

In this fun game, players go in alphabetical order beginning with *A*, stating name, spouse's name, place they came from and what they sell. Each thing they say must begin with that letter. For example, the first player might say, "My name is Alice; my husband's name is Albert; I come from Alabama; I sell applesauce." Second player might say, "My name is Billy; my wife's name is Brenda; I come from Boston; I sell beans." Play continues. When a player can't respond, that player is out. Surviving players continue.

Noah's Ark

A game that always adds laughs and excitement to any children's party, this one requires an even number of players — the bigger the group, the more the hilarity. Each player is paired with a partner; the idea is that they act as two of the animals that lived on Noah's ark. Players should select animals that make a noise that they can imitate, such as pigs, ducks, chickens, sheep, cows, frogs, turkeys, horses, dogs, cats, etc. One player from each pair is blindfolded, and the partners all scatter around the room.

Then these players immediately make sounds representing the animal they chose to be, attempting to attract the blindfolded partner. This feat is most difficult because of the overwhelming variety of sounds. The players making animal sounds must not move or walk toward their blindfolded partner. The first couple to reunite wins, and play resumes with players pairing off with different partners and choosing different animals to represent.

Numbered Chairs

Kids never tire of playing this popular party game. It's lots of fun when at least 16 players participate. Chairs are placed in a circle. One player takes the number-one chair and is the *leader*; chairs are numbered to the left of the *leader*, from two to however many players are in the game. Chairs must all be occupied. Players must constantly concentrate because after a while they will have a new number, different from the one first assigned to them, and they must always respond immediately when their present number is called and must say another player's number.

The game begins when the *leader* calls a number, for example, "eight." Number eight must promptly call a number, such as "twelve," and this player quickly calls another number, etc. The game continues until a player fails to respond or hesitates. For example, if number twelve slips up and doesn't react when his or her number is called, he or she must move to the last chair to the right of the *leader*. (If there are sixteen players, player twelve then moves to chair sixteen. Every player from thirteen to sixteen must then move to the right. Player thirteen becomes number twelve and so on down to player sixteen, who then assumes the number fifteen.)

After affected players have assumed their new seats, the *leader* calls out a number, as in the beginning, and play continues with players promptly calling out another number after their number is announced. Players may call "one," the *leader's* number, and if the *leader* messes up by failing to answer immediately, the *leader* moves to seat sixteen and all players after him or her move to the seat on the right. Player number two then becomes number one and acts as *leader*, calling out a number whenever any player fails to respond correctly. Whenever a player responds promptly, he or she calls out a different number.

Players always find this game challenging because the numbers constantly change and it gets quite confusing.

One Potato, Two Potato

This delightful game has enchanted children for many, many decades. Players hold out their clenched fists, thumbs up, and the child designated as the *caller* taps each fist in turn, counting:

> One potato,
> Two potato,
> Three potato, four.
> Five potato,
> Six potato,
> Seven potato,
> more!

The *caller* begins by first banging his or her right fist on left fist and left fist on right fist, continuing likewise around the group. When *caller* says "more," the player hit must place that fist behind his or her back. When a player has had each fist hit on the word "more", that player is out. If the *caller* counts his or her own fists out, the *caller* continues to call and count around, excluding himself or herself, until one player remains with clenched fist. That player is the winner and becomes the next *caller*.

Pass the LifeSaver

This games never fails to liven up a party. Two or more teams line up, one team member behind the other, each player clenching a toothpick in his or her teeth. The first player on each team has a LifeSaver candy on his toothpick. On the signal to start, the first team member attempts to pass the LifeSaver to the second and so on down the line, using the toothpick. Players may not touch the LifeSaver as it is being transferred from one toothpick to the next. The team who passes the LifeSaver to the end of its line first is the winner.

Penny Pastime

This unusual little pastime is a sure bet when it comes to getting a smile from kids. Once they learn it, they take the greatest pleasure in performing it for their friends and family members because it makes them feel smart. It works best with children six and older. Five pennies are used. Ask the child to open one of his or her hands widely, palm up. Place the pennies — one by one, Lincoln's head showing — on the child's palm where they remain until the end. After each penny is placed, ask the child the questions that follow, in order, and then tell them the correct answer. Here is how it goes:

ONE penny:　　QUESTION: See any perfume?
　　　　　　　ANSWER: There's a cent. (scent)
TWO pennies:　QUESTION: See any fruit?
　　　　　　　ANSWER: There's a pair. (pear)
THREE pennies: QUESTION: See any snakes?
　　　　　　　ANSWER: There's three copperheads.
FOUR pennies:　QUESTION: See any cars?
　　　　　　　ANSWER: There's four Lincolns.
FIVE pennies:　QUESTION: See any candy?
　　　　　　　ANSWER: Are you kidding? Not nowadays for five cents!

Pickup Sticks

A centuries old game that many believe originated in China, this was played with sticks made of ivory. Kids find this game fun and challenging. Pickup sticks are still sold in stores today and come with assigned values, but straws, swizzle sticks or plastic stirrers can also be used. A table or floor is used as the playing surface.

After the first player holds the sticks in a bunch in one hand, he or she lets them drop. Then this player attempts to pick up the sticks one by one, being careful not to disturb any of the other sticks. When the player removes the first stick, he or she can use it to assist in picking up the others by pressing the end of the next stick with his or her first stick, making is easier to remove from the pile.

Whenever a player moves another stick, it's the next player's turn. If a player has chosen a stick to go after, he or she can't change and go after another one. Players collect sticks throughout the game. If playing with a store-bought set of pickup sticks, the player with the most points wins after all sticks have been picked up. When playing with regular straws or swizzle sticks, the player with the most sticks at the end is the winner.

Pin the Tail on the Donkey

Kids have fun playing this game, which has been popular at kids' parties for years and years. A cardboard figure of a donkey without a tail is hung on the wall. Players line up behind one another in front of the donkey. The first player is blindfolded, handed the donkey's tail and turned around several times. The player tries to pin the tail in the correct spot. Then the next player is blindfolded and takes a turn.

The game continues until all players have taken a turn. Players who pin the tail in the right spot get a small prize. If no one hits the exact spot, the player who comes closest wins.

Puss in the Circle

Younger children are especially fond of this tag game. It requires a large circle drawn on the ground. Players stand in a circle behind the line while one player, *puss*, stands in the middle. *Puss* may tag any player who steps even one foot inside the circle. All the players call out, "Can't catch me," teasing *puss* as they step in and out of the circle. When *puss* tags any player who steps in the circle, this player then joins *puss* in the center trying to tag the others. The last one remaining untagged wins.

Puss in the Corner

An old-time favorite, this game is fun at a party or at any time. Be ready for lots of laughs in this one. Players each choose a corner or a spot in the room where they stand. Everyone has a place except one player, *puss*, who stands in the middle. Whenever *puss* says, "Puss wants a corner," players must change places with another player. *Puss* runs and tries to get into another player's spot. If *puss* does, then the player left without a place becomes *puss*. If *puss* doesn't get a spot, he must go back to the center, wait a few minutes and call again.

Questions

Youngsters giggle a lot in this game because of the goofy answers to the questions asked. Players divide into two equal sized groups, each having a *leader*. Questions and answers are written down beforehand. The *leader* of one group gives each player in his or her group a question written on a piece of paper. The *leader* of the other team gives an answer written on a piece of paper to every player in his or her group.

The game begins when the first player in the question group reads his or her question, and the first player in the answer group responds with the answer he or she was handed in the beginning. The result causes laughter every time. For example, the question might read: "Why do birds fly south for the winter?" the answer could be: "The Dodgers won the World Series."

Remember

Children have a chance to use their memory skills in this game. About 20 small objects — such as a spool of thread, bottle opener, comb, button, safety pin, paper clip, etc. — are placed on a tray. No item should be too large, since it would be too easily remembered. Players gather around the tray and have one minute to look at the objects. After the minute is up, the tray is covered. Players have three minutes to write down as many objects as they can remember. When time is up, the tray is uncovered again. The player who remembers the most items wins.

Simon Says

Kids have been delighting in this game for hundreds of years, and it's still a hit today. A leader acting as *Simon* tells players what feats to perform, for example, "Simon says sit down." If *Simon* doesn't say "Simon says" at the beginning of the assigned task, players should not do it. The game is more exciting if *Simon's* instructions are announced quickly. Whenever players follow an instruction not preceded by "Simon says," they are out. The last player left is the new *Simon*.

Stop, Thief

Kids always get a thrill out of playing detective games. The player chosen as *thief* is sent out of the room. Then the other players choose a *detective* . Players and the *detective* all join hands and form a large circle around a hat. Everyone moves slowly clockwise. The *thief* returns, entering the circle by touching two joined hands, takes the hat and tries to exit the circle before the *detective* tags him or her. Since the *detective* may go after the *thief* within the circle, the *thief* must quickly grab the hat and dash out of the circle by opening it in the same way as before (touching two joined hands). Once outside the circle, the *thief* is safe, and the *detective* is the new *thief*. If caught, he remains the *thief*.

Tell the Smell

This interesting pastime gives kids something to sniff at. Ten different substances that can be identified by their smell are selected, for example, coffee, licorice, vanilla, oranges, vinegar, cloves, moth balls, garlic, chocolate, cinnamon, bananas, onion, rose petals or lemons. Each item is put in an unidentified bottle. All the bottles are numbered. As the bottles are passed around, players sniff and write down what they think the item is next to the corresponding number. The player correctly guessing the greatest number of smells wins the game.

This Is My Nose

Kids love playing this silly pastime, which tests their concentration and coordination. All children sit in a line facing one player, who is *it*. While taking hold of his or her own ear, *it* points to one of the players and says, "This is my nose," and counts to ten. This player must hold his or her nose and respond, "This is my ear," before *it* finishes counting to ten. *It* continues pointing to other players one at a time, announcing another body part while touching a different part of the body.

The player pointed to must touch the part of the body *it* calls out while saying, "This is my____" (the part of his or her anatomy *it* is touching). Any player who fails to respond correctly in either way or within the count of ten is out. The last remaining player is the next *it*. When *it* acts quickly, the game is most amusing.

Touch It

Kids get a kick out of this game, which always livens up a party and tests their memory. Each player is blindfolded. The parent of the child hosting the party has a tray containing approximately 20 or more common small household items, for example, pen, nail clipper, nail file, pocket calculator, comb, screwdriver, button, paper clip, etc. As the tray is passed to each player, he or she touches the objects one after another. When the tray is taken from the room, each person is given a sheet of paper and a pencil. Players are allowed three minutes to write down the items they touched on the tray. The player who has recorded the most correct articles is the winner.

Up, Jenkins!

Kids like this game, in which quickness and coordination are necessary. Two teams sit facing each other on either side of a table. Teams choose *captains*. One team passes a quarter under the table from team player to another.

When the opposing team *captain* says "Up, Jenkins!" all hands must quickly be raised above the table. On "Down, Jenkins!" all hands are slapped down, palms flat on the table.

The player holding the coin tries to disguise its sound as it hits the table or get it down without any noise at all. The opposing team *captain* and team members discuss which player is concealing the quarter and signals the chosen player to raise one hand at a time. The hand with the quarter must be the last ordered up. If correct, the opposing team gets the quarter and play resumes. If incorrect, the same team tries again. Each time a team loses, it chooses a new *captain*.

Where's the Leader?

Children always enjoy this active game. One player acts as *it* and leaves the room. While *it* is gone, a *leader* is chosen. Other players follow the actions of the *leader*. For example, the *leader* might begin by waving a hand. When *it* returns, everyone is waving a hand. About five seconds later, the *leader* slyly starts another action for the others to perform. The *leader* continues changing actions every five or ten seconds. Whenever *it* discovers who the *leader* is, the *leader* becomes *it* and leaves the room, and a new *leader* is chosen.

Who, Sir, I Sir?

This is an exciting memory game and rhythmic game. Children love to play it again and again. At least five players are needed — the more there are the greater the fun. Each player is assigned a number. One player acts as the *leader* and tries to keep the game and chant going at an increasingly faster speed, attempting to eliminate players one at a time by confusing or surprising them into giving a wrong answer or not answering at all.

The game may be accompanied by a clapping rhythm set up by the *leader*. The others follow the rhythm clapping. Players sit in a circle, and the *leader* assigns each player a number. The *leader* begins by saying: "Someone has stolen my hat. Have you seen my hat?" pointing to a player. This player jumps up, and the following conversation begins:

PLAYER: Who, sir, I, sir?
LEADER: Yes, sir, you, sir.
PLAYER: No, not I, sir!
LEADER: If not you, sir, who, sir?
PLAYER: Seven, sir! (or any number that has been assigned to a player)

Number seven jumps up quickly and goes through the same conversation with the leader beginning at "Who, sir..." The game continues, with the pace getting faster and faster. The last player left to answer the leader's question is the winner.

Zoom

School-aged children find this game both challenging and exciting. Players sit in a circle with the player designated *it* in the middle. *It* points to a circle player, says a three-letter word, such as "dog," and spells it out. Then *it* counts to ten and says, "Zoom." The player pointed to must name items beginning with each of the letters in the word, for example, "Doughnut, owl, geese." When the child pointed to responds correctly before the word "Zoom," *it* then points to another player, says another three-letter word, and the game continues. If a player pointed to fails to name three objects by the time *it* says "Zoom," that player becomes *it*.

Index